STRENGTH
OF THE HILLS

UNDERSTANDING SCOTTISH SPIRITUALITY

STRENGTH
OF THE HILLS

JENNY ROBERTSON

Published by
The Bible Reading Fellowship
First Floor, Elsfield Hall
15–17 Elsfield Way, Oxford OX2 8FG
ISBN 1 84101 125 8
First published 2001
1 3 5 7 9 10 8 6 4 2 0

Acknowledgments

Unless otherwise stated, scripture quotations are taken from the *Holy Bible,
New International Version*, copyright © 1973, 1978, 1984 by International Bible
Society, are used by permission of Hodder & Stoughton Limited. All rights reserved.
'NIV' is a registered trademark of International Bible Society.
UK trademark number 1448790.

Scripture quotations taken from The New Revised Standard Version of the Bible,
Anglicized Edition, are copyright © 1989, 1995 by the Division of Christian
Education of the National Council of the Churches of Christ in the USA, and are
used by permission. All rights reserved.

Extracts from the Authorized Version of the Bible (The King James Bible),
the rights in which are vested in the Crown, are reproduced by permission
of the Crown's patentee, Cambridge University Press.

Translation from Scots by Jenny Robertson unless otherwise stated.

A catalogue record for this book is available from the British Library

Printed and bound in Great Britain by
Omnia Books Limited, Glasgow

CONTENTS

CHAPTER I

The Far Side of the Sea

If I rise on the wings of the dawn, if I settle on the
far side of the sea, even there your hand will guide me,
your right hand will hold me fast.

Psalm 139:9–10

All too frequently Scotland is described in the same terms as England. But Scotland's story differs from England's. It is the same with Christian Scotland. The Scottish Churches speak—and sing—with their own voice.

Strength of the Hills will try to catch something of the colour and tone of Scotland. It highlights the main events in two millennia. This first chapter sets the scene and gives an overview of what is to come.

Ideal homes

David longed for water and said, 'Oh, that someone would get me a drink of water from the well near the gate of Bethlehem!' So the three mighty men broke through the Philistine lines, drew water from the

ACKNOWLEDGMENTS

There's a sense in which I grew up with this book, but in the actual writing I needed to check facts and find out more in areas where my knowledge was weak. In fact, this book could not have been written without the generosity of friends old and new. First of all, my thanks to Naomi Starkey of BRF for 'birthing' the book.

Sister Claire Wardaugh of the Society of the Sacred Heart in Edinburgh kindly passed on papers by Father Mark Dilworth and Father Anthony Ross. Father Andrew Monaghan, Radio Forth, topped me up with *God's People*, the book of a 1991 radio series. Revd Steve Butler, Rector of St James' Episcopal Church, Leith, embodies in his ministry the music and inclusivity of the Iona Community. He also lent me his copy of *Chasing the Wild Goose*. Thank you, Steve! Revd Shirley Fraser of St George's Tillydrone in Aberdeen lent me books, gave advice and went the length of posting them to Poland. I know that she and other friends who pray supported this book with unbreakable threads.

Another minister, Norma Stewart, newly retired from Queen's Park Church, patiently dealt with my phone call while removal men were clearing her manse. She put me in touch with Miss Jean Bain, who was kind enough to send me the report of her church's visit to Budapest included in the Appendix. From Budapest itself, Ruth Colclough and Pearl Harrison sent faxes and e-mails and, together with the minister of the Scots Kirk there and his family, Revd Ken MacKenzie and Mrs Jane MacKenzie, gave me hospitality. Kenneth MacDonald, who, after a lifetime lecturing in Gaelic has been ordained into the Church of Scotland's ministry, shared books and ideas. Revd Timothy Morris, Dean of the Scottish Episcopal Church in Edinburgh, found time in a heavy workload to update me on the situation of that Church. Thank you, Tim!

Xanthe Robertson became my daughter-in-law while I was working on this book. She guided me into the Parish Church in Restalrig—and I have to thank her minister, Revd Ewan Aitken, for patiently answering my questions and sending me the booklet by the Revd

Notman. Xanthe opened the doors of Simpson House to me as well, and her team leader, Douglas, gave me time, tea, information, a guided tour and useful literature. My thanks to them.

Backing me up and answering all my questions about facts and dates was Stuart. Thank you, dear husband! My brother-in-law also e-mailed answers to my questions about Scots and lent me books. Thank you, Peter.

Fearghus MacFhionnlaigh let me invade his home via the tele-phone, shared his exposition of the tower of Babel and let me use it in this book.

Dr Joe Donnelly of Glasgow University, a consultant in economic history in Warsaw, shared his specialist knowledge of money matters within the medieval Church, old liturgies and breviaries and much else besides.

And finally, thank you, Donald and Rachel Meek. You opened your home and your library. Your vision, erudition and generosity, shared with gentle humour and great courtesy, leave me, quite literally—and perhaps it's no bad thing—'lost for words'.

well near the gate of Bethlehem and carried it back to David. (2 Samuel 23:15–16)

We all have our own image of 'home', and we hope that heaven may include it. In David's case the longing to drink not any water, but 'water from the well near the gate of Bethlehem' was stronger even than thirst. For some people the ideal place, the place for which the exile longs, might be an orchard of gnarled apple trees: the taste of home is in the smell of an apple. Russian friends in tower blocks in Moscow and St Petersburg long for a wooden house in a forest clearing with berries and mushrooms to be gathered and lapping lake water close by. For Scots the wooden hut becomes 'Granny's hielan' hame', a small white house cradled by hills of heather. This 'ideal home' often looks out to sea. The 'strength of the hills' (Psalm 95:4, AV) is in Scotland's story, and so is the sound of the sea.

In Irish legends 'the far side of the sea' is the place where life is renewed—the realm of those who never grow old. *Tir-nan-Og* it is called in Scots Gaelic, 'the land of the young'.

We know that there is no such place: west of mainland Britain lie the Hebrides, with Ireland to the south and America beyond. Yet sunset over still waters; a smudge of an island, lifting for a moment on a far horizon; a wind-tossed seabird silhouetted against lowering clouds; white spray breaking—all speak of 'the far side of the sea'. They are in the psalm which sings to us from the open pages of our Bibles.

WESTWARD WOAD! WHO WERE THE 'CELTS'?

You foolish Galatians! (Galatians 3:1)

Ancient Greek historians mention 'Celts' and 'Galatians'—thus tenuously linking 'Celtic' tribespeople and farmers with the Galatians to whom Paul wrote his epistle. However, the peoples of Britain and Ireland did not call themselves or their languages Celtic: that was the name given them by Roman and Greek imperialists and geographers. Their accounts of the peoples of Gaul (France) and Britain gave rise to legends of the 'noble

Gaul', of the 'warrior Celt', the honourable barbarian. The concept of the barbarian Celt—however honourable—stuck and, as we shall see, it influenced English-speaking policies, ministry and mission in the Highlands until the 19th century. At that point landowners shipped the bulk of their Gaelic-speaking tenants away.

The Celtic languages of Europe have survived least in the areas where Roman control was most complete and where literacy first spread. But the Romans failed to conquer the west of the British Isles or Ireland. Scots and Irish Gaelic and Welsh are still spoken as native languages. Scotland has never been monoglot. Basically, because language, community and culture are linked, the question we should ask is not 'Who are the Celts?' but 'Where are the Gaelic-speaking people of Scotland?' This book will answer that question.

Here now is a brief explanation about the native languages of the British Isles. Broadly speaking, the languages of Britain at the time of the Roman invasion of its southern seashore were Celtic: Brythonic (British) and Goidelic (Irish). These two branches of the Celtic language (both descended from Indo-European) are also known as P and Q Celtic. If this seems hopelessly complicated, think of the place name Penrith, and compare it with the name of Malcolm Canmore, the 11th-century king whose marriage to the Saxon princess Margaret brought Scotland into contact with Norman feudalism. 'Pen' and 'Can' both mean 'head': the one is Welsh (Brythonic, or P Celtic) while the other is from Scots Gaelic (Goidelic, or Q Celtic).

Brythonic is the parent language of Welsh, Cornish and Breton. Scots Gaelic and Manx stem from Goedelic—Irish Gaelic. There was one other known language in Scotland, spoken by people north of the River Forth, whom the Romans nicknamed the Picts—the painted ones—because they tattooed their bodies with blue dye called woad. Pictish was most probably a P Celtic language, although some scholars still maintain that, like Basque, Pictish represented the non-Indo-European tongue of some very early inhabitants of the area. There were many native tribes in the area the Romans called Caledonia. The Picts were probably an amalgam of tribal groups living north of the Forth-Clyde isthmus who resisted the advance of Roman legionaries and raided their outposts as far south as

Hadrian's Wall. Traces of Pictish remain in place names in eastern Scotland to this day.

The Celtic peoples of ancient Britain have left their legends and even their songs. When we sing, 'Bye baby bunting, daddy's gone a hunting...' we could be echoing a song which found its way into the 'Goddodin', an early epic poem. The poem was written down in the 13th century, but the text is far older, and this lullaby strayed into a section about battles and killings:

> When your daddy went off to hunt,
> Spear on his shoulder, club in his hand,
> He'd call the hounds so swift of foot...
> He'd strike fish from a coracle...
> Bring back a stag, a boar, a roe...[1]

The epic 'Gododdin' was carried into Wales by Brythonic speakers from the Lothians (the area around present-day Edinburgh). So we see that in the early years of the Scottish story—and indeed up until the 16th century—we can't think in terms of a divide between north and south, or Scotland and England. Links were strong between the Lothians, Strathclyde, Galloway and Wales; and, after the sixth century, between Ireland and the Gaelic-speaking area of Scotland, often known as the *Gaidhealtachd*.

In the medieval period, however, divisions became more sharply focused within Scotland; chroniclers began to distinguish between Highland and Lowland culture, dress and language. The three main languages of Scotland in the medieval period were Latin, Gaelic and Scots. The nobility—and this includes the Gaelic-speaking clan chieftains—would also have been fluent in French. Scots is a cousin of Anglo-Saxon. Some people argue that it is a distinct dialect of the Germanic parent; others that it is a language in its own right. Scots has regional variations. For example, the Scots of the north-east is different from that of the Lowlands, often called 'Lallans'.

Orkney and Shetland have their own linguistic forms of English, though the dialect Norn, which was Norse as opposed to Germanic, died out in the 19th century.

Language is an issue in Scotland in a way that it is not in England. The churches have had a significant part to play, and may still have, as we shall see in Chapter 10.

THE BEGINNINGS OF CHRISTIANITY IN BRITAIN

All authority in heaven and on earth has been given to me. Therefore go and make disciples of all nations. (Matthew 28:18–19)

Christianity came to southern Britain on the heels of the Roman legions, who invaded in AD43. Christianity became the official religion of the Roman Empire following the baptism of the Emperor Constantine in AD337, and the Church began to enjoy enormous prestige. Christianity spread along the commercial routes of a Roman world which was threatened but had not yet collapsed, which may explain how the faith first came to Galloway in south-west Scotland.

But Rome itself was under threat: barbarian tribes attacked the city in AD410. Caesar's soldiers, who had built forts, walls, roads and cities all over southern Britain, turned back to defend their imperilled Empire.

Incoming Saxon warlords looked at Roman ruins with awe. They were sure that no mortal man could have erected these columns and facades, splendid even in dereliction, and so they supposed that a race of gods had once lived upon the earth and put up the buildings, which their armies now avoided for fear of ghosts.

THE FOURTH AND FIFTH CENTURIES: PATRICK AND NINIAN

Take heart! I have overcome the world. (John 16:33)

While Anglo-Saxons were overrunning the east, the old Romano-British ways clung on in the west—and with them remnants of the Christian faith. Two names shine out. Both are British-born: one is Patrick, the other Ninian.

Patrick was born around AD410 on the western coast of Britain, maybe as far north as Dumbarton. His father was a Christian deacon, but Patrick, on his own admission, found his faith in naked extremity 'at the far side of the sea'; for at the age of fifteen he was captured by pirates and sold as a slave in Ireland. There, in misery, with no hope of freedom, he recited half-remembered prayers and God became real to him: he took Christ as his breastplate, the Holy Trinity as his shield. The chance to escape came, and Patrick seized it. Safely back at home, however, he dreamt that he heard 'the voice of the Irish' calling to him, 'Come and walk among us.' He accordingly set out to take his former captors captive for Christ. He returned to Ireland around AD460 and his long life took him to the last decade of the fifth century. Patrick left an autobiography, and this piece of writing helps us to date his life and work.

The same kind of Romano-British heritage, some half a century earlier, nurtured Ninian of Galloway (his name probably comes from a scribe's misspelling of 'Nynia'). Ninian is known from an eighth-century account, *Miracula Nyniae Episcopi* (*Miracles of Bishop Nynia*), and from Bede, monk of Jarrow in Northumberland, who died in AD735. Bede's great *History of the English Church and People* (which includes stories of the Christian faith north of the Border too) is a major source for the sixth century, just after the time of Ninian and Patrick. Bede mentions Ninian only as an aside in his description of the life and work of St Columba of Iona, but states that it is thanks to 'the preaching of the Word by that reverend and saintly man, Bishop Nynia' that the tribes of southern and eastern Scotland had 'given up the error of idolatry and received the true faith.'[2] According to Bede, Ninian spent ten years studying in Rome and was consecrated bishop before he set out on the long and hazardous journey back to his homeland. En route, Ninian stayed in Gaul with St Martin, Bishop of Tours, whose spirituality leaned towards the hermit life of the Fathers of the Egyptian desert. He then returned to Galloway.

Ninian's ministry is traditionally said to have spread north and east, across the Rivers Clyde and Forth, into Pictland. A Latin praise-poem written in the eighth century by a monk at Whithorn eulogizes the saint's mission:

What can I say that is worthy of you, Bishop to be revered in the world, or who is able to compose hymns to do justice to you, who successfully gave the commandments of Christ to the nations, teacher everywhere revered, after you obtained the multitudes of Picts for your own?[3]

Little is known of Ninian's Pictish mission. Place names may give a clue. Eccles or Egles, deriving from the Latin (and ultimately the Greek) *ecclesia*, 'church', can be found all over the area that Bede describes as having been converted by Ninian. 'Ninewells' also probably derives from St Ninian's name. There is a Ninewells Hospital in Dundee, for example. Also in Dundee, Sinavery (or Sinivee) Well—the name probably being derived from Ninian—is in the Caird Park between a 16th-century castle and a far older church, both ruined. A spout of water gushes from the rock-face beside the church and has never been known to run dry. Another Ninewell is to be found on Finavon Hill in Angus.[4]

These names from Dundee and Angus occur in the heart of Pictland—but they most likely attest later devotion to Ninian in the seventh century. So while Ninian doubtless used his excellent Roman connections to spread the gospel in Galloway, the Clyde Valley and the Lothians, the Picts remained largely an alien, pagan people, un-conquered by Rome and largely unswayed by missionary endeavours from Whithorn.

It was left to Columba of Iona to embark upon the conversion of Pictland almost two hundred years later. The Celtic missionaries from Iona absorbed whatever Ninian and his disciples may have planted. There is good scriptural backing for this: the grain of wheat which falls into the ground and dies produces much fruit (John 12:23–24). Bede suggests that Columba's missionary achievements in the Pictish heartland were built upon the foundation laid by Ninian and his unknown monks. Moreover, a very early stone font with traces of Pictish carving has recently been discovered. Dated around the fourth century, the font bears silent witness to the early spread of the gospel among the Picts.

WHITHORN—A PLACE OF PILGRIMAGE

Come, let us sing for joy to the Lord; let us shout aloud to the Rock of our salvation. (Psalm 95:1)

Bede explains that Ninian caused to have built (perhaps assisting in the work himself) 'a church of stone in the manner to which the Britons were not accustomed'. This church was dedicated to St Martin, showing the warm feelings that Ninian had towards the Bishop of Tours, whose compassion he seems to have copied in his own life among the hills of Galloway.

The church was known by its Latin name, *Candida Casa*, the white house. Bede, however, also gives it in his own Saxon speech: *hwit herne*, Whithorn. It has been said that while there is a White House in Washington and another in the Kremlin, the White House in Galloway is far more ancient![5]

The eighth-century Latin poem in praise of Ninian (mentioned above) says:

He was the first to lay the white foundations of a shining house and raise the venerable roof of the lofty temple, where the father, for all time sparkling in the brilliance of his mind, shone forth, a perfect splendour like a star... This is the house of the Lord which many are eager to visit, or many who have been afflicted with a disease of long-standing hurry there... Yet the divine grace in the saint's body could not die and be buried in earth's bosom, but it began to spread far and near, running through the ranks of the faithful and shedding light on the generations through many ages.[6]

Ninian's church may have been of white, shining stone but he, tutored by Martin, loved to withdraw into lonely places: a cave associated with Ninian in Luce Bay, near Whithorn, remains a place of pilgrimage to this day. It is tempting to conjecture that his Christianity had come wind-driven 'on the wings of the dawn' from the heartland of the desert: the life and lore of the Desert Fathers were surely close to Ninian's heart.

To reach Whithorn from Scotland's capital, Edinburgh, take the road south-west. You soon find yourself driving through peaceful countryside with the Pentland Hills rising on the right. Unimaginable aeons ago, violent geological activity created this landscape. Hills reared up towards the sky and released huge wedges of land which slipped downwards to make great valleys, while fire formed crystals, metal ores and different kinds of stone.

Travel by car shields us from the elements, fast roads carry us through villages so picturesque they invite us to linger, but we press on, passing ancient hill forts and old stone cottages with thick-set walls and well-groomed gardens. A shepherd drives sheep towards their fold: a white curve undulates across the hill. Horses graze in tranquil pasture.

In times gone by, horse power transported folk to and from Edinburgh along tracks frequently rendered all but impassable by weather. Wealthy travellers traversed these glens and hillsides. Further back in time, the kings and queens of medieval Scotland gave rich endowments to the centuries-old shrine of Ninian, which grew into a vast church with a large monastery complex. It became the fashionable thing to go on pilgrimage to Whithorn.

Robert the Bruce (d. 1329) set the royal fashion, believing himself cured of leprosy at the shrine, and thereafter the Stewart kings and queens travelled there with great ceremony and style, horse-borne in lurching litters. It's recorded that Queen Margaret, wife of James III, and her six ladies-in-waiting were all attired in chic new clothes of absolutely the latest mode for the pilgrimage, while James IV (1488–1513) brought harpists and pipers, a huge retinue which had to be housed and fed. Poorer pilgrims went on foot. They wore special badges: lead mined in the hills surrounding the Clyde valley was cast in the shape of small cockle-shells in which were fitted minuscule flasks for holy water or a sliver of relic bone.

However, stressing Christ's promise to be with the 'two or three gathered in his name' (Matthew 18:20), the Reformers later erased crucifixes, relics, holy water, saints' days, stained glass and festivals from the churches of Scotland. Pilgrimages were forbidden by law and the focus of attention in country places as well as in cities became the open Bible;

the Lord's Day, or Sabbath, drew folk in their Sunday best to Kirk (the Scots word for 'church') to sing their psalms and hear a lengthy sermon.

The great church and monastery complex at Whithorn fell so completely into disuse that there is almost nothing left. The pomp and pride of kings had made a beautiful church rise here to the glory of God—and, it was devoutly hoped, for the eternal well-being of the donors. The great church can never be rebuilt, but recent archaeological discoveries made by the Whithorn Dig give us an idea of its immense importance and former grandeur. Experts have also uncovered an invaluable record of social history, for the dig revealed evidence of the diseases of belly and bone from which the poor suffered—and the remedies of the monks who tended them.

Some of the earliest carved Christian crosses in Europe, dating back to the fifth century, are on display in the museum at Whithorn. The oldest, from around AD450, has a Latin inscription: 'We praise you, O Lord.' Further west still, in the Rhinns of Galloway, equally ancient stone crosses lift weathered heads to the hills and gather into their silence the sound of the sea.

THE WONDER AND TERROR OF THE SEA DRAWS PEOPLE TO ANCIENT HAUNTS OF HOLINESS

If I rise on the wings of the dawn, if I settle on the far side of the sea, even there your hand will guide me. (Psalm 139:9–10)

These words ring out as a statement of affirmation and joy which underlines the faith of strict Sabbath-keeping ministers on the one hand and a groundswell of creativity, even mysticism, on the other.

Although the sound of the sea on a summer's day is full of delight, in a gale the waves have ferocious claws and cruel wings. But for all that, the sea draws us. Its eternal movement stills our busyness. Its vastness dwarfs our self-importance. The sea silences the clamour of our voices. Our focus is carried to far horizons—and back to the point at which we began the quest beyond ourselves into the depths of sea-sound and silence. The sea takes us out and brings us home. Perhaps that is why the first missionaries sought far headlands and impossible rock-faces where seabirds roost, and why people are still drawn to these ancient haunts of holiness. For although Ninian's church had been demolished and the ministers of the Reformed Kirk fined anyone caught at the old superstitious practice of pilgrimage, Whithorn had been such an important spiritual centre that people kept on visiting the cave associated with the saint. Some carved their names and the date of their visit on the rough rock-face, leaving a record the years have not defaced—the graffiti dates back to the 18th century.

Nowadays, when church buildings have been closed—or turned into craft centres, museums or garages—the wheel has turned full circle: for once again, people seek out remote places for picnic or for pilgrimage. Some scratch a loved one's name on pebbles flung up by the sea. These small tokens of prayer are left on ledges in St Ninian's cave where ancient carved crosses once stood. The cave looks out to five kingdoms: the Isle of Man, Ireland, the Mull of Galloway, England—and, it is said, the kingdom of heaven. People still come here to do their own thing before God. Catholic and Protestant, the old differences forgotten, make their pilgrimage across the rocky shore and enter the cave, which is marked by a plain wooden cross. Stripped of ceremony, faith draws those who travel light along life's road. There is no organ, no chanting of choirs, but the silence is filled with the sound of the sea, the song of the wind and the seabirds.

Here, once again, we are with the psalmist in his flight 'to the far side of the sea'. A century and a half after Ninian, Irish monks chose the 'white martyrdom' of exile for the sake of the gospel. They used this term to distinguish their witness from the ultimate sacrifice made by martyrs who suffered and died for their faith, but old Irish texts reveal that the monks often found their self-imposed exile costly. There seems no end to the tale of these unknown women and men of faith who left the comfort of the hall and the harp for the perils of the ocean, coverings of down for beds of birch and heather root. This book can never do justice to the subject. As the monks themselves would say, the ocean is immense and the craft so frail—but we shall attempt to paddle at the edges of ancient seaways.

AN OVERVIEW OF SCOTLAND'S STORY UNTIL THE REFORMATION (1560)

A time to be born and a time to die... a time for war and a time for peace. (Ecclesiastes 3:2, 8)

The fifth, sixth, seventh and eighth centuries were a time of growth for the gospel in the land we now call Scotland. Small military aristocracies jostled with one another for ascendancy—some Brythonic speaking; others Saxon, others Gaelic and others Pictish. Christianity sat very lightly on some of them. The epic poem, the 'Gododdin', already referred to, praises 'Tudfwich Hir' who 'would slay Saxons at least once a week' and exalts 'the battle leader... His gauntlet is raised against pagans and Gauls and Picts'.[7]

However, Christianity did exert a unifying force. When the English king of Northumbria occupied parts of southern Pictland in the seventh century, there was no clash between the churches, as the Northumbrians had been converted to Christianity by St Aidan from Iona. The English missionaries therefore had the same church structures as the Christian Picts of the Columban Church. Controversy arose, however, over the date when Easter should be celebrated and over the shape of the monks' tonsure (the Iona Church followed ancient druidic practice and shaved the front of the head from ear to ear). The Synod of Whitby, in 664, chose the Roman form of Christianity. Roman Catholicism had come to Canterbury from Rome in 597, 34 years after Columba's arrival in Iona and the same year as his death. As we look at Scotland's story we shall see how the Catholic faith gradually supplanted the Columban form as Scotland entered the early Middle Ages. Feudal nobles of Norman lineage began to vie for power in a land which still espoused ancient tribal ideals of kingship.

Then in the 16th century came the Reformation, taking a different form and course from the one imposed on England. The English King Henry VIII had been forced into conflict with the Papacy because he wished to commit official adultery. In Scotland, although the monarch,

Mary Stewart (also known as Mary, Queen of Scots), remained a convinced Catholic, the Reformation was made a *fait accompli* by an act of law in 1560. The structures in the Scottish Reformed Church made a complete break with the old hierarchies of bishops and patronage which were preserved south of the Border.

THE SCOTTISH KIRK AFTER THE REFORMATION

Remember the Sabbath Day by keeping it holy. (Exodus 20:8)

The clergy in Scotland are known as ministers (servants). The minister in her or his own parish serves as one among the elders. The core governing group of each parish church is the Kirk Session, which in turn is answerable to the local presbytery. The presbytery, which includes the minister and representative laity, gives its name to the church: 'Presbyterian'. (The Anglican Church in Scotland is called Episcopalian, or the Scottish Episcopal Church.) The presbytery deals with local business while each May the General Assembly meets in Edinburgh, to be presided over by a Moderator who is elected for a year.

In the 17th century, James I (or James VI of Scotland), his son Charles I and grandson Charles II unwisely tried to impose episcopacy on Scotland. Much bloodshed ensued and later chapters will take up this story. However, all was not gloom and doom.

John Knox, the preacher of the Scottish Reformation, had set out his principles of church structure. The *First Book of Discipline* (1561) also arranged for 'a school in every parish'. As we shall see, literacy resulted from the widespread availability of the scriptures; and the reading of the Bible imbued each person with a sense of his or her own worth before God. There may have been some 'Holy Willies' (or hypocrites: the name comes from a poem by Robert Burns, about an elder who tries to ingratiate himself into the Almighty's good books), but the Scottish Church was a place of simple holiness.

To this day, in a Highland church I look at the rain-spattered windows as we sing the psalms, and the ancient faith of Israel takes root all over again. When the singing stops, the bleating of sheep is heard and the cry of circling gulls—and we are with David on the hills of Judah. We are with him as we sing the 23rd psalm to the tune Crimond; like him we 'lift our eyes to the hills' and sing, 'Behold he that keeps Israel, he slumbers not nor sleeps' (Psalm 121:1, 4, metrical version).

For almost five centuries the Scots Kirk, in its various Presbyterian forms, involved the whole community. The faith was as rugged as the landscape, as rugged as the congregations who wended their way in all weathers to sit long on wooden pews, hear lengthy expositions of the scriptures and sing the psalms. Hard though the walk might have been on winter Sabbaths when blizzards drove across the moors, it was difficult in summer too, for then the sun shone on enticingly blue water, and Sunday best prickled uncomfortably—but woe betide anyone who played truant!

Presbyterianism was strict and patriarchal. The pulpit took the place of the altar in the centre of the church and was set high above the pews—in country parishes it was on a level with the laird's (landowner's) pew; nevertheless the minister remained a member of presbytery, one among the elders. As we have seen, the name reminds us that she or he is a servant.

The Kirk defined Scottish culture for centuries. It told Scots folk that this is 'oor ain'—it is not English—and so it gave the northern kingdom its unique identity. As a Scottish institution, the Church of Scotland sustained the concept of a distinct Scottish nationhood (not nationalism) and helped to compensate for the sense of inferiority which had rankled ever since 'the lion beat the unicorn all about the town', as an old nursery rhyme puts it. For although the red lion rampant flies proudly on Scottish flags, the symbol of Scotland is the unicorn—a fabled creature, fearsome, yet fey. It could be gentled by a young girl and would guard small, frail things—but remain for ever free. The Authorized Version of the Bible renders Job 39:9 as follows: 'Will the unicorn be willing to serve thee? Will he stand all night by thy crib?' And the unicorn is willing, for the crib contains the Saviour of the world.

So Christianity found faithful adherents in Scotland and this book will show how their faith was renewed throughout the generations. There will be bigotry and pain, there will be great love and homely trust, a deep sense of being 'called', and a clear-cut response. There will be missionaries and martyrs—even as late as the 20th century.

The Church is prayer and worship; the Church is also people. We shall meet memorable characters on our journey and cover many miles as well as centuries. Sometimes our route will take us to the 'far side of the sea'; much of it will be through hills and rough country. But 'the strength of the hills is his also' (Psalm 95:4, AV)—and this is what undergirds the Scottish Christian story.

CHAPTER 2

COLUMBA & IONA

'A Jewel of Silver in a Silver Dish'

A word aptly spoken is like apples of gold in settings of silver.
PROVERBS 25:11

The flame of God's love dwells in my heart
Like a jewel of silver in a silver dish.[8]

The striking imagery of this Latin prayer attributed to St Columba also aptly describes the island of Iona, the cradle of Christianity in Scotland.

The Isle of Iona is, most people would agree, far more than a place. You may visit it only once in your lifetime, but you never forget it. You may go back year after year, and every time find that lift of the heart as you approach the shore. Iona is literally 'a jewel of silver in a silver dish': the sparkling silver sand of the island's tranquil bays is lapped by 'the silver dish' of the sea.

You approach Iona via Bunessan on Mull. Here, Mary Macdonald (1789–1872) composed a hymn whose tune, 'Bunessan', is well known as the setting for *Morning Has Broken*. The lilting notes of the melody as well as the poem's theme of new beginnings are a good introduction to the isle of Iona.

The island was first recorded as Hy, or I. A scribe later made a slip of the pen and misplaced the genitive case, Ion. It was a happy mistake producing a name which resonates with the man most associated with the island, Colum-cille, Columba of the Church. For, as Columba's biographer and kinsman, Adamnan, the ninth abbot of Iona, explains, Columba in Latin and Iona in Hebrew both mean 'dove'. Yet Columba (c. 529–597) was soldier as much as monkish scribe, prince as much as priest. His ability to curse was as legendary as his power to bless.

Columba's life is known from very early Irish texts and poems written in both Latin and Irish Gaelic. In the seventh century, Abbot Adamnan (the name is variously spelt) composed an elegant biography in Latin, entitled *Life of St Columba*. Adamnan was writing in the aftermath of the decisions of the Synod of Whitby (664). This Synod had challenged the leadership of the Iona church and Adamnan was at pains to redress the situation. In highlighting miracles attributed to Columba, Abbot Adamnan skilfully lifts the saint from the tensions which had beset all branches of the Church at that period. Instead, against the backdrop of a remote island with its storms and tempests, its windblown birds, he presents an enduring picture of a simple man of God:

Angelic in appearance, graceful in speech, holy in work, with talents of the highest order, and consummate prudence; he lived a soldier of Christ for thirty-four years on an island... beloved by all, for a holy joy ever beaming on his face revealed the joy and gladness with which the Holy Spirit filled his inmost soul.[9]

Adamnan shows Columba as prophet and pilgrim, at ease with 'men of lower rank', thieves and peasants as well as with kings. His record also gives authentic glimpses of domestic life—marital problems, family love and feuds, seafaring and the constant danger from raiders and robbers. Thus, among the monsters and miracles, the biography paints a unique picture of Scottish life in an era condescendingly known as the Dark Ages. Adamnan's *Life of St Columba* has been called 'the most complete piece of such biography that all Europe can boast of, not only at so early a period, but even through the whole Middle Ages'.[10]

Columba was born in Donegal on 7 December. His father was connected to the ruling house of Ireland, a branch of which had crossed the Irish Sea to Dunadd in Argyll, western Scotland, to colonize the kingdom of Dalriada. His mother, Eithne, was also descended from Irish kings.

Columba's early life was dedicated to the study of the scriptures. He quickly acquired a reputation for holiness but, in spite of this, as an aristocrat from a race of warriors, he was imperious and quick-tempered. The professor of Celtic in Aberdeen University, Dr Donald Meek, relates that while Columba is known as *caomh* (gentle) in the Hebrides, in Donegal he is altogether a more sinister figure. On Tiree, Professor Meek's own birthplace, a rock devoid of seaweed is a lasting legacy of the saint's power to curse.

But in this he was a man of his culture and time. 'Primitive Irish ecclesiastics, and especially the superior class, commonly known as saints, were very impatient of contradiction, and very resentful of injury,' writes Dr William Reeves in his Introduction to Adamnan's *Life*.

COLUMBA'S MISSION SPREADS CHRISTIANITY AND IRISH LANGUAGE TO SCOTLAND

Come, my children, listen to me; I will teach you the fear of the Lord. (Psalm 34:11)

In AD563, when he was 42 years old, Columba chose the 'white martyrdom' of exile and set sail eastwards from Derry. The legend is that he and his twelve companions sailed until they could see Ireland no more, and that Columba landed on Iona but longed for his native land on 'the far side of the sea' for the rest of his days.

In fact, politics and necessity mingled in Columba's decision to take the pilgrim's path eastward. Ireland was only a day's sail away and over the years Columba made several return visits. As we have seen, Irish chiefs, kinsmen of Columba's, had already colonized the area of Dalriada, on the west coast of Scotland. The Latin word for a speaker of Irish was *Scotus*: thus Irish expansion gave Scotland its name. The colonizers, including Columba and his monks, also brought their Irish language, which developed as Scots Gaelic.

Not unpredictably, given his family connections there, Columba initially made Dalriada his Scottish base. The Irish Annals record that King Connall of Dalriada approved the donation of the strategically situated island of Hy (Iona) to Columba as a foundation from which to start missionary work eastwards into Pictland, thrusting up to Inverness.

THE LOCKED GATES OF A PICTISH FORT
FLY OPEN BEFORE COLUMBA

And I tell you that you are Peter, and on this rock I will build my church, and the gates of Hades will not overcome it. I will give you the keys of the kingdom of heaven; whatever you bind on earth will be bound in heaven, and whatever you loose on earth will be loosed in heaven. (Matthew 16:18–19)

The stories woven around Columba's mission tell of confrontations with druids, of magical contests, of causing the winds to change their course and of a cowed pagan king, Bridei (Brude), meekly accepting conversion. Adamnan describes how Bridei, the pagan Pictish king in Inverness, 'elated by the pride of royalty, acted haughtily, and would not open his gates on the first arrival of the blessed man'. Columba, who walks through the pages of Adamnan's *Life* much as St Peter does in the first twelve chapters of the book of Acts, made the sign of the cross over the locked doors, knocked—and the gates flew open, allowing Columba and his companions to pass through.

The reality is that Bridei gave Columba peaceful entry into Pictland and formally confirmed his possession of Hy—but Adamnan's biography shows that the conversion of Pictland was not easy. Columba, it seems, did not know the Pictish language. His Pictish converts 'learned through an interpreter the word of life preached by the holy man'.

The powers of darkness, represented by the druids, by storms and monsters, had to be overcome. Adamnan records that the druid Briochan, no less a person than King Brude's foster-father, raised a storm against Columba. Darkness fell and great winds whipped Loch Ness into a fury. Columba, however, 'called on Christ the Lord and embarked in his small boat; and whilst the sailors hesitated, he the more confidently ordered them to raise the sails against the wind'. Astonished onlookers watched Columba's coracle sail against the wind the druid had raised.

All this is well and truly in the style of ancient Irish legend. To modern readers of Adamnan's biography, the magic may seem contrived, but Columba's mission of liberation was rooted in his faith in the Christ of the scriptures. And so was his care of new converts. For example, one of the children of a newly baptized peasant family fell ill and died. The druids taunted the bereaved parents, saying that this proved that the druidic gods were stronger than the God of the Christians. Columba 'burned with zeal for God' and hurried to console the grief-stricken household.

There, like Peter at the bedside of Tabitha, Columba 'prayed to Christ our Lord, having his face bedewed with copious tears. Then rising from his kneeling posture he turned his eyes towards the deceased and said, "In the name of the Lord Jesus Christ, arise and stand upon thy feet."' The boy was restored to life. Columba led him outside and 'the cries of the applauding multitude broke forth, sorrow was turned into joy, and the God of the Christians glorified'.[11]

COLUMBA AS SPIRITUAL FATHER AND FRIEND OF THE POOR

Blessed are the merciful. (Matthew 5:7)

Stories abound of Columba's kindness to the poor, of his accepting frugal hospitality and returning it a hundredfold with gifts and blessings. Adamnan also tells of a woman who refused to sleep with her husband because she did not love him. The couple sought Columba's help. Columba (by this time Abbot of Iona) pointed out to the woman that, according to scripture, she was denying her own body, since husband and wife are 'one flesh'. However, the woman stood her ground. She informed the Abbot that she was ready to do anything except share a bed with her husband. This is by no means the only incident in the Scottish story when a woman forthrightly challenges an ecclesiastic! Columba neither argued nor scolded. He suggested that all three of them should 'join in prayer to the Lord and in fasting'. The couple agreed and they all prayed and fasted for the rest of the day. However, instead of going to bed, Columba continued to pray for the couple: 'The following night the saint spent sleepless in prayer for them,' says Adamnan. Next morning the woman told him, 'The man whom I hated yesterday, I love today; for my heart hath been changed last night in some unknown way—from hatred to love.'

This revealing encounter points up qualities which explain why Columba remains central to the Scottish Christian story. There are stories too of his having a vision of a particular emergency—of a battle, perhaps —going against some of his spiritual children; or of monks who were wearied with hard toil, or of pilgrims beset by storms at sea, or a kinswoman in hard childbirth. In every case Columba immediately hurried to his cell or chapel and wrestled in prayer on behalf of those in distress. Columba's gifts of prophecy enabled him to see death as well as blessing (but if the people concerned were Christian, then, of course, death was indeed a blessing).

In his portrait of Columba, 'the dove of the Church', Abbot Adamnan created a compelling picture of a man of great holiness whose prayers 'changed pure water into true wine'. The friend of angels, those 'bright hosts' who favoured him with their 'sweet and most delightful society', Columba is perceived as a saint for all Christians. Catholic, Episcopalian and Presbyterian churches are dedicated to him.

However, it may be that some of Columba's aura belongs to his biographer, Adamnan himself. Professor Michael Lynch in his award-winning study, *Scotland: A New History*, describes Adamnan as 'the most self-effacing of all Scottish saints' and suggests that Adamnan rather than Columba was the true apostle to the Picts. His abbacy (679–704) marked the high point of Iona's mission. Dedications reveal the spread of Adamnan's influence. Linked, like Columba, by birth to the Irish aristocracy, Adamnan seems never to have forgotten that the gospel is also to the humble and weak. His most important diplomatic achievement is his 'Law of the Innocents', promulgated at the Synod of Birr which Adamnan convened in County Offaly in 697, following a vision of the Virgin Mary who urged Adamnan to speak up for women on behalf of the host of heaven.

The Law, which protected women, children and clergy from having to fight in war, was secured by a list of guarantors from Ireland and Scotland —including Pictish Scotland. 'These guarantors gave three shouts of malediction on every male who would kill a woman with his right hand or left, by a kick, or by his tongue, so that his heirs are elder, nettle and the corncrake,' writes a contemporary chronicler, who further explains:

The work which the best of women had to do was to go to battle and battlefield, encounter and camping, fighting and hosting, wounding and slaying. On one side of her she would carry a bag of provisions, on the other her babe. Her wooden pole upon her back. Thirty feet long it was, and had at one end an iron hook, which she would thrust into the tress of some woman in the opposite battalion. Her husband behind her, carrying a fence-stake in his hand and flogging her on to battle. For at that time it was the head of a woman or her two breasts which were taken as trophies.[12]

It must be remembered that, just as a great artist attracted a school of painters, much Christian enterprise attributed to a major name like those of Columba or Ninian was, in fact, the work of other missionary monks. So any assessment of Columba should include the work of brother monks. Brendan, for example, who navigated the North Atlantic and discovered the goodness of God in the dangers of the deep, also founded monasteries in Hebridean islands. His contemporary Moluag chose the Isle of Lismore, near Oban, for his base, and there are plenty of legends to underscore the power of his mission. Dedications to St Donan, too, are found right across northern Scotland, from Caithness to the Isle of Lewis. Beautiful Kildonan in Sutherland bears his name and the most photographed Scottish castle, Eilean Donan, also bears witness to him. Donan's community on Eigg rivalled Iona, and Donan and his monks were martyred there in 617, supposedly on the orders of a jealous queen. The monks were murdered before the altar as they celebrated Mass.

The charismatic Maelruba founded an important centre in Applecross. Dedications to Maelruba show that his missionary work was extensive, reaching all over Wester Ross into Skye, and north and east as far as Dingwall. His grave at Applecross is called Cladh Maree—and beautiful Loch Maree is called after him. He is said to have been murdered by Vikings in 722 and, says the *Aberdeen Breviary*, written by Bishop Elphinstone in the 15th century, a chapel of oak was built on the site of Maelruba's murder which later became the parish church of Urqhuart.

Many and marvellous are the stories of these saints. Something of the lingering cult of Maelruba was found when the presbytery of Dingwall visited remote Highland parishes in 1657 and found that 'amongst their abominable and heathenish practices, the people (of Applecross) were accustomed to sacrifice bulls at a certaine time, upon the 25th of August, which day is dedicate, as they conceive to S. Mourie, as they still call him'.[13]

It is important to remember that Columba, towering genius as he was, was a man of his time, perhaps more than half a pagan still. A storm at sea, gentle breezes, a storm-tossed bird, the old white pony which foretold the saint's death, spoke powerfully to him of forces which we perceive now only in hints of folklore. Columba's monastery on Iona was not just a spiritual powerhouse and the hub of a missionary enterprise which extended from Ireland to Pictland. It was also part of a wealthy, sophisticated culture which could support great works of art. It was a close-knit, Irish-focused community modelled on secular kingship and kinship.

COLUMBA AS SCHOLAR AND FRIEND OF ANGELS

He spoke with an angel; he studied Greek grammar.[14]

Angels are often present in Columba's story. A hill close to the abbey he founded on Iona is called 'Hill of the Angels', *Cnoc Angel*. Sometimes when he prayed in seclusion, light spilled out 'through the chinks of the doors and keyholes'. These 'sweet visits', says Adamnan, mostly took place during winter nights when Columba was keeping solitary vigil and 'the lovely and tranquil aspect of the holy angels' filled the saint with joy.

It is well known that Columba transcribed the scriptures by hand: Adamnan records that he was working on Psalm 34 when he died in the year 597. A Gaelic elegy written just after Columba's death praises the saint's scholarship and learning: 'He spoke with an angel; he studied Greek grammar...'. The poet also shows how the Christianity of Iona was intertwined with the Church at Rome and Byzantium when he adds: 'By his mighty skill he kept the law firm. Rome was known... He applied the judgments of Basil... By his wisdom he made glosses clear. He fixed the Psalms, he made the books of Law known, those books Cassian loved.'[15]

LINKS AND TWISTS IN THE TALE

Their voice goes out into all the earth, their words to the end of the world. (Psalm 19:4)

The reference to Basil and Cassian links Columba with the Fathers of the Eastern Church.

When Adamnan was Abbot of Iona at the end of the seventh century, a galley returning from the Holy Land was blown off course and was wrecked on the shores of Iona. The monks rescued the shipwrecked pilgrims. Although the shipwreck had happened when Adamnan was 'daily beset by laborious and almost insupportable ecclesiastical business from every quarter', he eagerly seized this unique opportunity to discover more about the world of the Bible, of St Paul and the prophets. One of the rescued pilgrims was a Gaulish bishop named Arculph, and his first-hand information about the Holy Land gave colour and added veracity to the scriptures. Adamnan carefully checked Arculph's account with a reference book of Bible place names in his monastery library; and he and his monks made a 'faithful and accurate' record of the holy places, based on Arculph's information. Adamnan's manuscript *About the Holy Places* (*De Locis Sanctis*) highlights the importance of the Bible in the life and work of the monks of Iona.

The Gaulish bishop, Arculph, grateful for his rescue and gratified by the monks' interest in his experiences, may well have left another souvenir—an ancient manuscript from the Middle East, the *Diatessaron*, a compendium of the Four Gospels. Art historians have pointed out that illustrations in this manuscript—a copy of which was presented to the Vatican by the Byzantine Emperor in the 15th century—were identical to those in the Book of Durrow, and strikingly similar to those in other Celtic Gospel books. The illustrations in the *Diatessaron* must have opened tremendous possibilities for the Iona artists. In his book *From the Holy Mountain*, William Dalrymple, citing a Danish art historian, Carl Nordenfalk, explains:

Although the styles of the Diatessaron and the two Celtic Gospel Books are very different—as you would expect from two manuscripts drawn centuries apart— the poses of the symbols, the angles at which they were drawn and the attitudes they strike are identical with each other, and totally different to anything else in Christian iconography. Moreover, both sets of manuscripts open with nearly identical full-page illuminations showing a double-armed cross embedded in a weave of intricate interlace. The same pattern also found its way onto a Pictish cross-slab, the Rosemarkie Stone, which still lies on the Beauly Firth, a few miles north-east of Inverness... Nordenfalk proposed, not unreasonably, that the arrival of the Diatessaron was the spark which ignited the almost miraculous blaze of Celtic book illumination during the seventh and eighth centuries, a process which culminated in such masterpieces as the Lindisfarne Gospels and the Book of Kells... It is a considerable cultural debt, and one that is little known, and certainly unrepaid.[16]

The great art treasure, the Book of Kells, which is now thought to have originated on Iona, also reveals the importance of the Hebridean island in the development of the cult of the Virgin Mary in the late eighth century. The first full-page illustration of the Virgin and Child is the earliest representation of Mary in Western Christendom. Indeed, even in the East, only a small image from Alexandria (around AD400) and a full-page representation in a late sixth-century Syrian manuscript are any earlier. Art historians conclude that Arculph may also have brought an awareness of these icons to Iona.

About the same time, a monk on Iona, Cu Chuimne (Hound of Memory), composed a hymn to the Virgin, one of the oldest examples of this kind of devotional liturgy in the West. These verses give us a fascinating glimpse into the daily worship of the monastery on Iona. We can guess how the chanting of monks, which Columba loved, must have sounded in performance 'in two-fold choir, from side to side':

> *Let us sing every day,*
> *Harmonizing in turns,*
> *Together proclaiming to God*
> *A hymn worthy of holy Mary.*

> *In two-fold choir, from side to side,*
> *Let us praise Mary,*
> *So that the voice strikes every ear*
> *With alternating praise.*[17]

'I SAW MANKIND'S LORD HASTEN WITH COURAGE TO CLIMB UPON ME'

And I, when I am lifted up from the earth, will draw all people to myself. (John 12:32, NRSV)

Missionaries from Iona converted the hitherto pagan Angles of Northern England. The spread of the gospel in Northumbria produced great stone-carvings; and a very important early English poem, 'The Dream of the Rood', dates from this period. Fragments of this great dream-poem are carved in runes on a magnificent stone cross, one of the oldest artefacts of Anglo-Saxon England, which stands inside the parish church of Ruthwell in Dumfriesshire, just across the Border. The top panel of the tall shaft cross depicts the hermit monks, Paul and Anthony, breaking bread. In her study of Anglo-Saxon spirituality, *High King of Heaven* (Mowbray, 1999), Benedicta Ward SLG points out that these two hermits appear on at least ten Irish high crosses, showing how interlinked the early English and Irish Christian influences were. The cross was a meeting place for Celt and Saxon. Both the runic poem and the cross itself are splendid examples of the art of Christian Northumbria.

THE CONTINUING NETWORKING OF THE GOSPEL

The wind blows wherever it pleases... So it is with everyone born of the Spirit. (John 3:8)

'The Dream of the Rood' describes Christ as a young hero. The Tree, the cross of Calvary itself, speaks:

> Men then hauled me on shoulders, until I was set on a hill;
> many foes then fastened me. I saw mankind's Lord
> rush with great courage to climb upon me.
> Then I dared not, against the Lord's word,
> bow or break, when I saw trembling
> the earth's surface. All those enemies
> I might have felled: yet I stood fast.
> Then the young hero stripped himself—that was God almighty—
> strong and steadfast. Bold in the sight of many
> he mounted the cross, since he would ransom mankind.
> I trembled when the Man embraced me.[18]

Soon the young warrior Christ captured the hearts and the imaginations of the pagan Vikings. In time they would produce saints—not least the gentle Earl Magnus of Orkney who, on Easter Monday, 16 April 1116, stood beneath the butcher's axe to win peace for his people.

The Norse seafarers in their dragon-prowed ships brought terror to the inhabitants of ninth-century Britain. Iona fell beneath their ravaging axes early in the ninth century. The records show that 86 monks were murdered, giving an indication of the size of the monastery at that period. However, around four hundred years after Iona was sacked, a Norse artist produced a small bronze bell-shrine, whose Christ embodies the nobility of the warrior-hero of the Ruthwell dream-poem.

The bell-shrine, which eventually found its way into the Royal Scottish Museum, was made in the twelfth century. The outer work covers earlier Irish silver, probably eighth-century. It was discovered in 1814 when a dry-stone dyke (a wall made of boulders with no cement) was repaired in the village of Kilmichael Glassary, in Mid-Argyll. The village looks out to the rocky fort of Dunadd, the capital of Dalriada where Columba had set up his base.

It should be explained that a bell-shrine doesn't ring. It encloses a reliquary. Its metal casing, however, is shaped like a bell. There is a handle at the top, and at the base is a small hole through which people could put a finger to touch the relic within.

The artist shows a Christ who is regal in suffering. His eyes are cast down; only the lids are visible. His shoulders are bare. His taut ribs show the stress his body is under; the tension only serves to deepen the dignity and resignation of his mien. The cloth fastened about his waist flows to his knees; great attention has been paid to the detail of the folds. On his head he wears not thorns but a king's crown.

Just such a figure, wearing a king's crown and with a similarly draped cloth, can be seen on the great doors of St Sophia in Novgorod, a great Viking city of early Russia. These doors were executed early in the 13th century, just a little later than the Kilmichael bell-shrine. Although the kingly crown remains a feature of Scandinavian portrayals of Christ to this day, the crown of thorns in fact made its first appearance in Christian art towards the end of the ninth century, showing how essentially conservative the Norse artists in Scotland were.

On the Kilmichael Glassary bell-shrine, above the head of Christ is a hand. Long fingers point down in priestly blessing, the thumb uppermost. It is the hand of the Father whose favour rests upon the suffering Son. Above the hand is a wavy line. Scholars conclude that this represents the wind—the Holy Spirit, the breath of God.

IONA—THE BURIAL PLACE OF KINGS

Foreigners will rebuild your walls, and their kings will serve you. (Isaiah 60:10)

The Scots king in Dalriada fled inland from the Vikings and, as a consequence, the two kingdoms of the Picts and Scots were eventually united under Cinead mac Ailpin (Kenneth MacAlpin) in AD847. Dunkeld now became the capital of Scotland, but Iona was still revered as a holy place and the burial place of kings. The Saxon Queen Margaret (c. 1040–1093) is said to have rebuilt part of the original monastery in the 11th century, including St Oran's Chapel, the oldest chapel on the island. In the 11th century, too, the king of Norway, graphically called Magnus Barelegs, made a pilgrimage to Iona.

Fifty years later, Reginald, Lord of the Isles, invited Benedictine monks to Iona and soon Augustinian nuns followed. During the medieval period the monasteries experienced times of corruption and decay (notably under Finguine, a notorious early 15th-century abbot), but also of renewal. Finguine's successor, the saintly Abbot Maol-Domhnaich, restored piety and prestige to Iona. Young men and women from Gaelic-speaking noble houses of the Highlands and Islands regularly became monks and nuns in Iona. The grave slab of Anna MacLean (an early 16th-century prioress of Iona), a masterpiece of stone-carving, bears witness to the affluence and culture which produced such rich art.[19]

In 1560 came the Reformation. The monks were forced to leave Iona (the nuns were left in peace for a little longer). The monastery buildings fell into decay, and the light lit by Columba seemed to have been extinguished. A thousand years after Columba had first set sail for Iona, one of his prophecies was fulfilled: 'Iona of my heart, Iona of my love, instead of monks' voices there shall be lowing of cattle.'

A small portable shrine survived the silence. Sometimes known as the Monymusk Reliquary, the Breacbennoch of St Columba is similar in shape to the much larger Pictish stone sarcophagus in St Andrews. *Breac* means 'shrine' and *bennoch*, 'blessed'. This small eighth-century house-shaped casket of beaten bronze and silver plates, less than twelve and a half centimetres long, is supposed to represent the Temple in Jerusalem and is said to have contained a relic of St Columba. Apart from Iona itself, the reliquary remains the most potent symbol of the political power and spiritual prestige of the Columban church. There is no Christian symbolism on the little box. It is Irish in form, resembling one of the small stone oratories of the Irish monks, but Pictish interlace swirls about the gold of hasps and handles.

There was an old tradition that this reliquary should be carried sunwise around the Scottish army before battle, and Robert the Bruce certainly had it carried ahead of him at the Battle of Bannockburn (1314). It passed into the hands of the Grants of Monymusk, and was still there early in the 20th century.

Bruce and the Breacbennoch are both depicted on twenty-pound notes issued by the Clydesdale Bank of Scotland, but the reliquary itself is tucked away behind museum glass in Edinburgh. Of greater significance to Scotland than the Sword of State which is displayed in the Crown Room at Edinburgh Castle, the reliquary provides a living link with Columba and is an emblem of Scottish kingship and of Christian devotion.[20]

'CHASING THE WILD GOOSE':
GEORGE MACLEOD AND THE IONA COMMUNITY

The kingdom of heaven is like yeast that a woman took and mixed into a large amount of flour until it worked all through the dough. (Matthew 13:33)

Faint stirrings of revival began in the 19th century, when Scotland became almost as important as Switzerland for the tours of the adventurous and the romantic. Tourists who braved rutted roads and wild seas to visit Iona included Dr Johnson, Keats and Wordsworth. In 1899, the Duke of Argyll gave the ruins of the abbey to the Church of Scotland. The gift was not only generous, it was also prophetic, for it came with a clause that the church should be restored for all branches of the Christian Church to worship there. But it was not until 1938 that the world at large began to be interested in Iona again.

Columba had set sail for Iona when he was 42 years old. In 1938, another 42-year-old clergyman set sail for Iona. The Revd George MacLeod was as passionate and controversial a figure as Columba himself. His concern was primarily for the deprived parishes of industrial Scotland. He had served for eight years in Govan, the Clydeside parish of shipyards and steelworks, all during the Depression. Distressed by the wastage of human skills in an area of high unemployment, George MacLeod set out to make the Church relevant to the needs of urban Scotland.

It was the eve of World War II and MacLeod, who had served with distinction in World War I, was now an avowed pacifist; but the new community, although all male, was to be neither celibate nor pacifist. The aim was to set up a training ground for young ministers who would then go and work in new housing schemes. 'Poverty is not our aim,' wrote George MacLeod. 'We only claim a privilege to make perhaps the sacrifices of those who work in really difficult places a little less acute.'[21]

The trainee ministers camped on the island and joined with craftsmen to restore the Abbey. After World War II, a gift of timber for the refectory arrived from Norway—an apology for damage done a thousand years before by Viking swords.

The Community began to exert an influence in places of need. Outstanding ministers, Geoff Shaw and Walter Fyffe, worked in the Glasgow Gorbals in the 1960s at a time when the area on the south side of the River Clyde was thought to be one of the worst in Europe. The Gorbals ministers attracted a unique circle of social workers and church workers. The group stressed the Church's role as servant, friend and prophet, especially in places of greatest need. They aimed to take Christ into the darkest streets of the city, to make friends with the friendless and to listen with patience to those who had no voice. Geoff Shaw finally moved into politics, dying at the age of fifty. He was no strident political campaigner, but a Christian who had made it his aim to live out the gospel.

Members of the Iona community went to India and Africa and brought a vision of simplicity to the affluent churches of the West. The songs of

Africa and the Caribbean are used in Iona worship and, through the work of the Wild Goose Worship Group under John Bell and Graham Maule, have percolated through to enrich mainstream churches. The Iona challenge is to 'apply on weekdays what we sing about on Sundays'—to be poor, disabled, unemployed: to be the Church wherever the Church is not. Sometimes the pilgrimage is not to but from Iona. In August 1999 a group of pilgrims against poverty sailed from Iona to walk to Westminster under the banner 'Walk for Change'. The walk was organized by Church Action on Poverty and the aim was to urge the Chancellor of the Exchequer, Gordon Brown, to establish a minimum standard of income. The pilgrims also hoped to waken the Church, the 'sleeping giant' as one of the walkers put it.[22]

'BUT ERE THE WORLD COME TO AN END, IONA SHALL BE AS IT WAS'

Columba had prophesied that the lowing of cattle would replace the monks' orisons. But his prophecy did not end there. 'Ere the world come to an end, Iona shall be as it was,' he foresaw. His language has died out on Iona, but now, once again, visitors and pilgrims come to Iona from all over the world. They find peace within the walls of the restored abbey church and on silver shores rinsed by the emeralds and amethysts of the sea. Many carry away a vision of the kingdom which began in Iona when God's warrior-dove came in the strength of the hills with a gospel which shook the centres of power, bringing hope to the poor and help to the distressed.

In the flowing of the tides of the Kingdom, Iona is once again as it was—and might it be that a community pledged to ecology and conservation, to adapting old ways to new issues, will find a place in its voice of prayer for Gaelic, the language of Columba? And then as the third millennium proceeds, not only the tune 'Bunessan', but its original words, will be understood once again on Mull and Iona.

CHAPTER 3

PICTLAND, TRIDUANA & RESTALRIG CHURCH

Blind in Body but Not in Soul

You say, 'I am rich; I have acquired wealth and do not need a thing.' But you do not realize that you are wretched, pitiful, poor, blind and naked. I counsel you to buy from me gold refined in the fire, so you can become rich; and white clothes to wear, so you can cover your shameful nakedness; and salve to put on your eyes, so you can see.

REVELATION 3:17–18

Bible events overlap with Scottish history in the sea journey of an improbable shipload of holy men and maidens from Colossae in Asia Minor to the shores of Fife. Colossae is linked with St Paul and his epistle to the Colossians, while the cargo carried by the fragile craft was nothing else but the bones—or some of them—of Andrew, the fisherman whom Jesus called from his work at the lakeside to become a 'fisher of men'.

The story of this sea journey may well be based on fact. Repeated waves of new arrivals have regularly beached upon the shores of Britain through-out the long history of human settlement. In Galloway, for example, generations of seafarers who had wintered further south sailed north to spend their summers on the beaches. These nomadic campers left their rubbish behind, enabling archaeologists to trace a way of life which pre-dated agriculture in the British Isles, going back to around 6000BC. Their boats differed very little from those later described by Roman military explorers and Christian scribes. A framework of pliant ash strengthened with sturdy oak was covered with ox hide and surmounted with a sail. These small boats could travel at speed and, upturned on the shore, weighted with stones, made good camping places.[23]

At the beginning of the Christian era, travel overland was dangerous at best, and mostly impossible. That intrepid traveller, the apostle Paul, lists an awesome catalogue of dangers: 'Three times I was shipwrecked, I spent a night and a day in the open sea, I have been constantly on the move. I have been in danger from rivers, in danger from bandits, in danger from my own countrymen, in danger from Gentiles; in danger in the city, in danger in the country, in danger at sea' (2 Corinthians 11:25–26).

Roads networked the Roman Empire, but inns were unsafe and robbers were many. And beyond the control of the legionaries, travellers had to contend with dense forest, hill and bog, wild animals—and wild people. So people went by sea. Trade, travellers, new ideas, new religions, invaders, all arrived first at coastal places and then percolated into the interior.

THE BEGINNINGS OF MONASTICISM AND THE HERMIT LIFE

Go, sell everything you have and… follow me. (Mark 10:21)

So we return to our holy travellers. The story goes that a Greek monk named Regulus had a dream in which he was told to arise and embark upon the white martyrdom, journeying he knew not whither, taking with him the bones of St Andrew the apostle. Now this part of the tale is not in the least far-fetched. Monasticism in the West owed its beginning to St Benedict and his monastery in Monte Cassino, but it ultimately derived from Egypt and the desert. A young man called Anthony started the trend in response to the command in the Gospel: 'Go, sell everything you have and give to the poor, and you will have treasure in heaven. Then come, follow me' (Mark 10:21). Two thousand years of Christianity have not made that command any easier; and yet all through the Christian story there have been men and women who have taken the command as literally as Anthony. These individuals seek solitude but never remain totally alone; however strictly they retreat, they exert an enormous influence. So it was that the joyful austerities of the hermits of North Africa reverberated to the far fringes of the known world, to Ireland and the Orkneys. On the small island of Stronsay in the Orkneys, for example, on a stunningly beautiful cliff walk you pass a geological fault—a geo or deep chasm, in which the sea churns endlessly. Then comes a stack, or pillar of ribbed stone, separated from the cliff face by tide and storm—and the walk leads to a broch, one of those fortified towers unique to northern and western Scotland and to Ireland. Before you reach this circular ruin, you teeter on the cliff edge to view a rocky arch which seems more like a perch for seabirds than for people. Here, incredibly, there was an early Christian hermitage.

So there is nothing surprising in the journey of Regulus. And it was only to be expected that he should have taken a holy relic—and what better than the bones of one of the apostles? What seems astonishing is that holy maidens should have travelled with the monks, but the legend says that they did, and that one of them was a beautiful girl called Triduana.

One version of the legend says that the ship was wrecked by a sudden storm, and Regulus and his party got ashore with nothing except the clothes they stood up in—and the casket with the precious relics of Andrew. Regulus built a church to St Andrew: the town of St Andrew's bears witness to it to this day. Triduana and her maidens seem to have left him at this point because we next hear of her in Forfar, where she sought a solitary place to pray—and where, alas, she attracted the (unwanted) attention of a Pictish prince, Nectaneus, or Nechtan.

THE ASCENDANCY OF THE PICTS, 685–850

He… sets me on my high places. (2 Samuel 22:34, NKJV)

The name Nechtan places Triduana in the eighth century, when the kingdom of the Picts was in the ascendant. It was by now a Christian kingdom—or at any rate the ruling class had embraced Christianity, as stone-carvings show. Political power was closely linked with the presence of a powerful cleric within the entourage of the king. Pre-Christian kings had been aided by their druids, who were thought to possess supernatural powers over nature. With the coming of Christianity, Columba and Adamnan had both drawn upon the Old Testament example of the prophet Samuel who had ordained and anointed first Saul and then David. A new, biblical theory of kingship was being evolved, as we shall see when we consider Pictish stone-carving.

Although Northumbrian rulers had pushed up the east coast of Scotland, taking Edinburgh itself, and had subjugated the Picts across the Firth of Forth, they were defeated by a Pictish king, Bridei mac Bile, at the Battle of Nechtansmere in 685. Their victory at Nechtansmere gave the Picts enormous prestige and they added to their success by gaining control of Dalriada in the west. Dalriada had been a centre for the Gaelic language and for the Irish church since the fifth century. Now the high fort at Dunadd, a natural rocky outcrop in Mid Argyll, fell into Pictish hands—or rather, feet. For on Dunadd, carved into the rock are two fairly deep footprints into which the ruler set his foot as a sign of overlordship. The footprints on Dunadd point north towards the noble peak of Ben (Mount) Cruachan, awesome when its bare head lifts free of mist or is flushed in a glowing sunset.

The strength of the hills surrounded the Pictish king as he stood upon the rock, his foot firmly in the carved print. Similar footprints are found elsewhere in Scotland and northern Europe and date from a very early period. However, at Dunadd, ogham script (an early alphabet based on a series of strokes either side of a line) and a Pictish boar were carved on the stone beside the coronation point in the seventh or eight century:

these pagan symbols plainly still had their place at the coronation of nominally Christian kings. Clergy with holy oil, psalm and prayer surrounded the king also, and perhaps he exulted with David, 'He makes my feet like the feet of deer and sets me on my high places' (2 Samuel 22:34, NKJV).

NECHTAN CONFRONTS TRIDUANA

If your hand or your foot causes you to sin, cut it off and throw it away... And if your eye causes you to sin, gouge it out and throw it away. (Matthew 18:8–9)

Nechtan became king of the Picts in 706 and reigned until 724, extending the power and prestige of Pictland by becoming overlord of smaller tribal units and high king over an area which extended from Dalriada, throughout present-day Central Region, Angus and the Mearns and Fife—a remarkable achievement. He was baptized as a Christian in 710. But with the new faith, the legend goes, Nechtan needed a queen who was both saintly and beautiful. News of Triduana's virtuous life in seclusion with holy maidens must have attracted him, for the story goes that he sent suitors to Triduana to woo her.

To overcome her qualms and persuade her that to consort with a prince was in keeping with the Scriptures, the emissaries may have quoted Psalm 45:11: 'The king is enthralled by your beauty; honour him, for he is your lord.' Triduana, however, asked what it was about her that the prince found so beautiful. 'The surpassing beauty of your eyes,' the messengers told her. 'What your lord asks of me he shall obtain,' Triduana loftily told the delighted courtiers. While they were congratulating themselves on the success of their mission, she retired to a secret place where she gouged out her eyes, transfixed them to a long thorn or wooden pin and returned to the messengers with her grisly offering and the proud command, 'Accept what your prince desires.'

Triduana then made her blind way south across the Forth to a quiet settlement close to the fort of Dun Eidin. It is now the parish of Restalrig in the north-east of Edinburgh. Here she devoted her life to fasting and prayer—and particularly to prayers for those afflicted with diseases of the eye. Her name became associated with a healing well, and Restalrig became a major place of pilgrimage. For hundreds of years people with problems of sight or diseases of the eye came from all over Scotland to pray to the saint. The church which rose beside St Triduana's healing well was richly endowed by kings.

The importance and popularity of Triduana might be attested by the fact that there is a healing well dedicated to St Trodden beside Restenneth Priory, where Nechtan was baptized. And an annual fair called St Troddans or Trodlins Fair was held for many centuries and is still observed in the town of Forfar.

Nechtan himself launched a period which has gone down in history as 'the golden age of the Picts'. Little survives in document form, except lists and lineages of kings. From these, historians have deduced that Pictish society was matrilinear—with the succession passing through women. This doesn't seem to imply any great liberation for women in society as a whole—simply that princesses were kept apart to breed kings. It's thought that the fort in Edinburgh on its high rock was at one time used as a place of seclusion for royal women. However, a hunting scene on one great carved stone found at Hilton of Cadboll on the Moray Firth, but now in the Royal Scottish Museum in Edinburgh, places a woman in a prominent position. She rides side-saddle on a splendid horse—a mirror and comb are also shown among the dogs and deer, the spears and shields, the huntsmen on horseback and the retainers who come on foot behind the lady, blowing their horns. It is thought that while the hunting scene acknowledges the status and wealth of noble patrons, there could be a deeper application of Christian symbolism which the aristocracy had clearly espoused: the Christian soul (could this be the woman?) is in pursuit of Christ, the deer.

Pictish society has produced no lasting literature—nothing to compare, for example, with the earliest English poem, 'The Dream of the Rood'. But what the Picts lacked in literature they had in abundance in stone. Powerfully executed pagan symbols and Christian art are found confidently carved on broken stones, on slabs and embossed crosses all over Scotland, having survived centuries of neglect. The Greek and Roman Empires had been all but wiped out, but on the edges of the world Pictish artists were carving in stone superbly executed designs, significantly contributing to the great Irish-Celtic re-birth of civilization and culture that spread east to mainland Europe.

The earliest Pictish symbol stones are unique in Europe—national monuments to a civilization about which little else is known. Some show a crescent whose curving lines are filled in with flowing patterns and intersected by two lines which make a large V. Other geometric figures make a Z shape, discs and double discs, crescents, serpent shapes and, mysteriously, a mirror and a comb. Much later the mirror and the comb became applied to an enigmatic, legendary figure—the mermaid. Could this be some folk memory of the meaning of symbols which defy explanation today? Some of these symbols survive on silver (for example, the hoard found on St Ninian's Isle in Shetland) and may also have been carved on wood or leather or bone. They certainly had significance for the artists who carved them and for their patrons. There are fourteen different symbols which are repeated over and over again.

Many early stones depict birds and animals. One in the Royal Scottish Museum in Edinburgh shows a duck and a fish. Most famous of all is the bull from Burghead on the Moray Firth. Other stone carvings show wolves, horses, boars, stags, eagles, snakes and a peculiar animal which has become known as 'the Pictish beast'—a version of Nessie, the Loch Ness monster, perhaps. We have seen that a Pictish boar was carved on the rocky ramparts of the fort of Dunadd, close to the footprints where the kings were crowned. All the carved animals are vital and alive, potent symbols of force and majesty. They are portrayed in motion, with the joints and muscles strongly etched. The artists were acute observers, totally in sympathy with the natural world and rightly self-confident and at ease with their tools and their skills.

Anglian monks who gradually penetrated Pictland copied the animal designs in illuminated Gospel books. For example, a Pictish 'biting beast' was found on stones dug up in Moray—identical animals process up the border of the stone slab, each one biting the back of the animal in front—and a very similar 'biting beast' appears in an illustration in the Book of

Durrow, thought to have originated in Northumbria. Nevertheless, there is a basic cultural difference between the two representations which has nothing to do with artistic skill. The Pictish stone-carvers understood the significance of the symbolic beasts, while the monks simply adapted the design from another culture.

By the eighth century, the old Iona-inspired monastic influences were being overtaken by Roman Catholic church structures, power being based around a bishop rather than an abbot. Nechtan himself, lord of the entire territory north of the Forth, adopted Roman structures within the native church, and planned to adorn Pictland with stone churches in the Roman style. He accordingly sent word to Jarrow, Bede's illustrious monastery in Northumbria, asking that architects be sent north for the purpose. This decision brought Pictland into mainstream European culture, via the Book of Kells and the Lindisfarne Gospels—whose work, as we have seen, is in turn influenced by the art of the Mediterranean.

The Pictish stone carvers were quick to draw upon these new sources of inspiration and incorporate them into their national heritage. The wealth of their carvings shows that there was a rich aristocracy who had readily embraced the Christian faith. They reveal that the processes of change that brought the Roman Catholic Church to Scotland were already at work. However, although the stone-carvers of Northumbria, Iona and Dalriada all produced marvellous free-standing crosses, Pictish sculptors continued to prefer stone slabs. A cross was carved on the face of the stone and on the reverse side might be battle scenes—as on the great cross in the churchyard at Aberlemno commemorating the Battle of Nechtansmere, which took place about ten kilometres away from the church. Thanks to the skill of an unknown artist, the event is depicted with historical veracity, high art and much drama. The defeat of the Anglian king Ecgfrith is clearly portrayed: he flees on horseback, casting aside his sword and shield, is opposed by foot-soldiers, faces the Pictish king and is killed. A raven on the bottom right of the slab eats his body. Such carvings are an invaluable source of information for historians: they reveal the shape of shields and weaponry, the type of clothing worn by senior clerics and important lords—and even their hairstyles and the cut of their beards.

OLD TESTAMENT REPRODUCTIONS ON PICTISH STONES

But David said to Saul, 'Your servant has been keeping his father's sheep. When a lion or a bear came and carried off a sheep from the flock, I went after it, struck it and rescued the sheep from its mouth...The Lord who delivered me from the paw of the lion and the paw of the bear will deliver me from the hand of this Philistine.' (1 Samuel 17:34–35, 37)

Other stone crosses depict hunting scenes, even sea battles, or scenes from the Bible with Pictish symbols adorning the base and sides. A favourite scene is King David snatching his sheep from the jaws of the lion, which he then slays. David is shown on the superb eighth-century cross at Kildalton in Islay, on which the Virgin and Child also make a first appearance. The David story is also depicted in St Andrews (taking us back to Regulus and the relics he brought across the sea), on an eighth-century shrine called the St Andrew Sarcophagus. This shrine pre-dates the cathedral and is a lasting testimony to a powerful Pictish church, influenced by the European mainstream but confidently employing its own native symbols. The sarcophagus is made of stone shaped like a large box. Carved panels show typical interlace, while the large front panel shows the scene in which David rescues his sheep. This story obviously appealed to the Pictish imagination: the design travelled north to the Moray Firth and thence across to Nigg in Ross-shire, where a great carved stone, dated between 800 and 850, shows the entire story of David. On a cross-slab from Aldbar, David grapples with a lion to save his horned sheep. His harp and shepherd's staff are shown on the stone—powerful symbols of peace, protection and, it may be, a love of music.

The David story had been taken up by Adamnan himself and skilfully intertwined into the rituals of kingship. In David there was a clear Old Testament model of a godly king, anointed with oil, warlike and brave, yet trusting the Lord; a musician with a legitimate succession instead of bloodshed. The Scottish belief in a divinely appointed king was to hold good even when King James moved to Westminster in 1603, explaining why, even in the 19th century, the humiliation of being merely 'North British' was tolerated in the light of the perceived greater good—obedience to the Crown.

THE LAST PICTISH STONES

Later Pictish stones show a mingling of Norse influences. The Viking terror hit the coasts of Britain in the ninth century and drove the centre of power inland. As we have seen, in 847 the King of Scots, Cinaed mac Ailpin (Kenneth MacAlpin), united the kingdoms of the Picts and Scots. He chose the Pictish centre at Scone for his inauguration ceremony. Tradition has it that he brought the famous Stone of Destiny there. This stone was later captured by the English under Edward I, and was returned to Scotland only in 1998, where it is now (controversially) placed in Edinburgh Castle.

MacAlpin also brought Columba's relics to Dunkeld, now the spiritual centre of the new kingdom. MacAlpin came from a branch of the ruling family of Dalriada—Columba's base—and the Gaelic Church, revitalized by his support, promoted Columba's language. The art of the symbol stones, no longer understood, died with the Pictish language. (New Age devotees have taken to adorning the old stones with flowers.)

The name of the new united kingdom—Alba—was first coined around the year 900. Under MacAlpin and his successors, a new territorial concept of kingship had replaced the tribal, people-focused name of Pictland. The Pictish peoples were completely absorbed by the Scots, leaving behind a legacy of land organization and place names: places beginning with 'Pit', or ending with 'o', are thought to be Pictish. They also left behind that rich heritage of stone-carving. Perhaps it is significant that the last great stone, Sueno's stone, rose to a tremendous height of 6.5 metres (21 feet). It is the swan-song of the Pictish stone sculptures, a carved poem of harmony and majesty. The enormous, heavily interlaced cross is set upon an interlaced slab. At the foot, now virtually defaced, but still regal in bearing, is the king with clergy and two saints, probably

St Andrew himself and St Columba. The Irish missionary has taken his place beside the apostle, the patron of Scotland whose bones Regulus bore with him centuries before, and the Pictish stone-carvers have used their art to bring glory to God and to Alba.[24]

CONTINUOUS WORSHIP AND INTERCESSION: THE WORK OF A COLLEGIATE CHURCH

I urge, then, first of all, that requests, prayers, intercession and thanksgiving be made for everyone—for kings and all those in authority, that we may live peaceful and quiet lives in all godliness and holiness. (1 Timothy 2:1–2)

The reminder of Regulus takes us back to St Triduana. Her well at Restalrig continued to attract pilgrims for centuries, and the Stewart kings desired to make the shrine into a great collegiate church in which prayer should be made continually for the peace of the realm and the salvation of the king and his family. In a collegiate church (there were four such churches in medieval Edinburgh and 38 in the whole of Scotland between 1342 and 1545), the clergy did not carry out pastoral work or parish duties but were solely concerned with worship, offering prayer continually and with great attention paid to music and singing. This kind of thinking was not purely spiritual. The number of masses said for the soul of a deceased relative (and paid for by the living) was believed to cut short the period spent in purgatory. Within this simplistic yet highly calculated view of the after-life lay the seeds of dissent which bore fruit in the Reformation.

But that was some way off, and Triduana's well was incorporated into an elaborately carved shrine on the lower floor of the Chapel Royal, a hexagonal building. During the reign of James III (1460–1488), Pope Innocent VIII issued a decree on 15 November 1487 that the church at Restalrig should become a collegiate charge under the jurisdiction of a Dean. The Dean had to be either a doctor of divinity or a doctor of canon law; the Deanery was under the direct jurisdiction of the Pope—proof of its prestige and importance.

Seven months later James III was dead—he fell at the Battle of Sauchieburn (11 June 1488)—and his son James IV ascended the throne. The new king was a lover of beauty (not excepting the female variety) and a generous benefactor. He continued the development of the collegiate church, making it one of the noblest and most beautiful of all Scottish churches, hallowed by prayer and honoured by the many pilgrims who came from all over Scotland to pray at St Triduana's shrine, as well as by the people of the parish of Restalrig who filled the great church on Sundays and holy days.

A RICH MEDLEY OF MUSIC AND WORSHIP

Sing to the Lord a new song, his praise in the assembly of the saints. (Psalm 149:1)

James IV guaranteed an income of 20 pounds Scots to be paid in perpetuity to the prebendary—or canon—who was to be skilled in music, both in singing and in the playing of musical instruments. The prebendary had to supervise a singing school and maintain two boys who would not only sing in the choir, but would also ring the bells for all the services, light the tapers and candles in the church, look after the fire in the prebendary's house and clean the church—all for eight pounds Scots each year. (A Scots pound was less than a pound sterling, but a Scots mile was longer than an English one: you got good value for your miles in Scotland!) A second prebendary was responsible for looking after jewels and ornaments, books and chalices, the keys of the church and the ornaments on the altars. Other church canons had to maintain the shrine and look after the offerings that people made to the saint. They all had to be good musicians and they were each given a room beside the church, together with a garden.

The liturgy was in Latin, and in this the Scottish Church was no different from anywhere else in medieval Catholic Europe. But the Scots vernacular was rich and vital. Folk who came to the shrine may well have prayed in their own tongue to 'Saint Tredwell… quhilk on ane prik has baith her ene' ('Saint Triduana who has both her eyes on one pointed stick'), that she might 'mend thair ene'.[25]

The Scots tongue reached a rich flowering in the 15th century when great poets, the Makars (makers), did for the language what Bach would do for music three centuries later. By now, English was becoming standardized and, thanks to Geoffrey Chaucer (1340–1400), the London form was showing all its potential as a great literary language. Scots, meanwhile, was also developing as an autonomous national language, clearly differentiated from London English in vocabulary and grammar. The comparison is sometimes made between Spanish and Portuguese, two very similar languages from a common source which gradually developed in their own ways.

Therefore, if we add all the richness of soaring Gothic architecture, music and colour with the Latin of the liturgy and the vigour of the Scots language, we have a bright picture of the shrine of Triduana in Restalrig. Her cult also took an up-turn in the 15th century as stories of half-remembered acts of holiness and legends were woven together to inspire kings and common folk alike.

The 16th century, however, opened with a major disaster. James IV and 10,000 Scots soldiers and lords, 'the flower of Scotland', perished at the Battle of Flodden in north-east England in 1513—a battle fought on behalf of France, Scotland's traditional ally against English troops led by the Earl of Surrey. It was a huge loss, robbing Scotland of leadership and vitality. James V was crowned in the aftermath of the defeat. His Coronation Mass was to be the last ever for a king in Scotland. Here is an abridged version of the Kyries from that Mass. Chanted antiphonally by two choirs, they must have transported the congregation to the high throne of heaven. I heard them at a concert given by St Nicholas Sang Schule, just one of many choirs and singing groups who are reviving the music of medieval and Renaissance Scotland:

Christ, King, high throned, the angels praise you with beautiful songs:
have mercy on your servants.
Christ, whom the church praises throughout all the world, whom the sun,
moon and stars, earth and sea serve for ever, have mercy.

O, dearest Child of the Blessed Virgin Mary, King of Kings, Redeemer of those you have purchased from the power of death with your own blood, have mercy.

The Dean of Restalrig and his feudal baron, Sir John Logan, had also perished at Flodden but James V, the father of Mary, Queen of Scots, continued to take a great interest in the collegiate chapel at Restalrig and honoured the next Dean with the title 'Guardian of the Scottish Church'.

But Restalrig's days of glory were numbered. Dr John Sinclair, appointed Dean in 1545, clashed with the reformer, John Knox, who described him as 'that perfyt hypocryte… blynd of ane eie in his body, bot of boith in his saule'.

On 21 December 1560, the first General Assembly of the Church of Scotland decreed 'that the Kirk of Restalrig, as a monument of idolatrie, be raysit and utterly casten downe and destroyed'.

The stern command was carried out to the letter. The great church and the hexagonal chapel above Triduana's well were pulled apart stone by stone. Only the east window and chancel walls remained. And in 1609 an Act of Parliament declared that the Kirk of Restalrig was to be 'suppressed and extinct from henceforth and for ever'.

And so it was done. Although the Reformation was initially relatively bloodless, all over Scotland great stone cathedrals fell before the axes of the Reformers—and fire and war, weather and plunder took a hand as well. From Whithorn to Elgin, from Melrose to Iona, abbeys and cloisters stood roofless and ruined. Cathedrals like that of St Giles in Edinburgh, St Mungo's in Glasgow and St Magnus' in Kirkwall were stripped internally and turned into parish churches. The annihilated parish church at Restalrig, however, was eventually given new life: in 1837 the present church building was erected on the site of the ancient one. Excavations in 1907 funded by the Earl of Moray uncovered Triduana's well in the undercroft of James III's chapel. A history of medicine in Scotland, written in 1927, states: 'Even now people with eye diseases come with bottles to collect the water.' Links with royalty continued when the Duchess of Gloucester planted a tree in the church garden in 1963. There is now a Society of Friends of Restalrig Church whose patron is the Earl of Moray. The glory of the medieval church has disappeared for ever and can only be imagined from fragments of stones which remain, but Triduana is still commemorated each year on 8 October when the Friends of Restalrig Church hold a concert of sacred music in her honour. And the parish church continues to serve the community. It is dedicated to St Margaret, whose story opens the next chapter.

CHAPTER 4

MEDIEVAL SCOTLAND FROM MARGARET TO MARY

'The Royal Way of the Cross'

How beautiful on the mountains are the feet of those who bring good news.

ISAIAH 52:7

When Pope Innocent IV canonized Queen Margaret, Scotland's only royal saint, in 1250, he said: 'A precious Pearl saw the light in Hungary, and lived at the court of the Confessor, a School of Holiness. Torn from homeland, you embraced another. You became Queen and Mother, the glory of the Scots. Your Queen's crown, a crown of Charity. Your way, the Royal Way of the Cross.'[26]

Edinburgh's much-visited Old Town is crowned by its famous Castle. The Royal Mile leads down from the Castle to the Palace of Holyrood, thus linking Margaret, whose chapel is still in the Castle, and Mary, Queen of Scots—two women whose lives, five hundred years apart, open and conclude the story of medieval Catholic Scotland (although Mary's reign actually coincides with the Reformation).

Both women have left a lasting legacy in Scotland's Christian story. Margaret, a Saxon princess, niece to Edward the Confessor of England, became Queen of Scotland when she married the King of Scots, Malcolm Canmore, in 1070. Mary, born in the Palace of Linlithgow in 1542, was crowned Queen of Scots at Stirling when she was nine months old, Scotland's last Catholic queen. She had already been promised in marriage to her young cousin, the future Edward VI of England, but the Scots lords broke off the engagement and Mary's uncle, Henry VIII of England, retaliated with seven years of war against Border towns, economic dislocation and enforced garrisoning of his soldiers in Scotland. The 'Rough Wooing' left Edinburgh and Leith in ruins and caused great loss in the local economies of Scotland. The Scots turned to their traditional allies, the French, and five-year-old Mary was betrothed to the Crown Prince, leaving Scotland for France where she married the young French prince when she was twelve. Widowed at 18, she returned to Scotland in 1561 in dismal weather. The Protestant reformer, John Knox, prejudiced against the young Catholic queen from the outset, read divine judgment in the swirling *haar*, or mist: 'The very face of heaven, the time of her arrival, did manifestly speak what comfort was brought into this country with her, to wit sorrow, dolour, darkness and all impiety... The sun was not seen to shine two days before, nor two days after.'[27]

Mary took up residence in the Palace of Holyrood where she romanced, danced, and created fine poems, providing a favourable ambience for other poets, including women. Her musicians made music—some pieces composed by the queen herself—and her courtiers committed crime. It was in the Palace of Holyrood that the Scots lords murdered her Italian secretary, David Rizzio, in front of the queen—she was pregnant at the time. Later Mary gave birth to her only surviving son, James VI (1567–1625), in a small wood-panelled room in the castle. It can still be viewed today. In her pain, Mary prayed to St Margaret of Scotland, queen like herself and mother of eight children. She asked for the saint's head and it was smuggled in—the Reformed Kirk forbidding such superstition—for Mary to touch. The last abbot of Dunfermline had hidden Margaret's relics and her body was eventually taken to Spain, where Philip II created a special shrine for St Margaret. After Mary's flight from Scotland in 1567, St Margaret's head was looked after by Bene-dictine monks, then by Jesuits, who took it to the Scots college in France. It seems to have disappeared without trace during the French Revolution.

Margaret herself had died in the castle, almost five hundred years earlier, on 16 November 1093. Weakened by years of austere fasting, suffering constant pain, Margaret attended her last Mass in the little oratory called now by her name, St Margaret's Chapel. She collapsed and was carried to bed. Her second son, Edgar—knowing that his uncle, Donald Ban, had surrounded the castle with troops, preparing to seize the throne—appeared at that moment to bring his mother news that her husband and eldest son had been led into a trap and treacherously killed in Northumberland. Seeing his mother so near death, the prince hesitated to tell her the truth. 'But,' writes her biographer, 'with a deep sigh she exclaimed, "I know it, my boy, I know it. By the Holy Cross, by the bond of our blood, I abjure you to tell the truth."'

She received the news calmly. Her biographer continues:

Feeling now that death was close at hand, she prayed, 'Lord Jesus Christ, who according to the will of the Father, through the co-operation of the Holy Ghost hast by Thy death given life to the world, deliver me.' As she was saying the words, 'Deliver me', her soul was freed from the chains of her body, and departed to Christ whom she had always loved.[28]

Under cover of swirling November mist, Margaret's body was smuggled out of the castle lest it fall into the hands of her enemies. Her faithful followers carried the queen's corpse, still with head and hair intact—her relics were only divided later—down the steep castle rock. Her third son, Etherlred, abbot of Dunkeld, had it taken to Dunfermline to be buried with dignity in front of the high altar of the church his mother had founded.

ST MARGARET'S CHAPEL—A PLACE OF PRAYER

Rejoice in the Lord always… Let your gentleness be evident to all. (Philippians 4:4–5)

St Margaret's Chapel is the oldest building in Edinburgh. It has survived the ravages of war and Reformation. Historical research in the 19th century re-discovered it—it was being used as a store for gunpowder. Set on the highest pinnacle of the Castle Rock, the little chapel was gradually restored and finally rededicated on 16 March 1934.

The Guild of St Margaret was created in 1942 to help maintain the chapel as a place of prayer. Margaret has remained a popular girl's name in Scotland and anyone with that name may join the Guild. Thus it is that the Margarets of Scotland bring fresh flowers to the chapel each week. Some of the Margarets active in the Guild also give out meal tickets for the homeless—an action their namesake would certainly have applauded.

The chapel is a great favourite for weddings—but brides should beware: the doorway is too narrow for full-hooped skirts!

MARGARET'S LIFE AND LEGACY

Therefore, as God's chosen people, holy and dearly loved, clothe yourselves with compassion, kindness, humility, gentleness and patience… and over all these virtues put on love. (Colossians 3:12, 14).

Margaret has gone down in history as a devoted wife whose husband, 16 years older than herself, genuinely loved her. She is known too as a mother of eight children, six sons and two daughters, who all survived into adulthood; and, above all, as a Christian queen who honoured and served the poor. She loved the scriptures. King Malcolm, her husband, set one of the Gospels she herself had illustrated into a silver cover for love of her. This Gospel Book is in the Bodleian Library in Oxford; a copy of the frontispiece is in the Chapel in Edinburgh Castle.

Margaret is also remembered by two small towns on the River Forth— North and South Queensferry. She provided inns on either side of the river and founded a ferry to take pilgrims across the river on their way to and from St Andrews: the ancient town was becoming increasingly popular as a place of pilgrimage and Margaret encouraged this trend.

Born in an age when queens are often no more than a name in royal genealogies, Margaret has a place in chronicles and histories in Britain and her native Hungary—and the books have flowed out steadily since her first authorized biography, written within a decade of her death. Margaret's second youngest daughter, Edith (or Matilda—the Norman French of England couldn't pronounce her Saxon name) had become Queen of England when her husband Henry I ascended the throne, uniting the Saxon and Norman dynasties. Educated at an English convent from early childhood, the new queen had hardly known her mother and was anxious that a biography should be written. A saintly mother would provide Matilda with good credentials in the royal court south of the Border. Margaret's spiritual friend and confessor, Bishop Turgot of St Andrews, readily complied.

Bishop Turgot's *Life of St Margaret, Queen of Scotland* was reissued in 1993, the 900th anniversary of Queen Margaret's death. At the same time the St Margaret's Chapel Guild commissioned an Edinburgh historian, Alan Wilson, to write a commemorative work, *St Margaret, Queen of Scotland*. It is to this work that I am indebted for many of the following facts of Margaret's life, especially the intriguing story of her origins.

KING STEPHEN OF HUNGARY:
NEW FAITH FOR A NEW MILLENNIUM

Do not forget to entertain strangers, for by so doing some people have entertained angels without knowing it. (Hebrews 13:2)

It is well known that Margaret was born in Hungary. The fact is attested in Hungarian archives and confirmed by many historians. It is not certain, however, that Margaret was related by blood to the royal line of Hungary. It might well be that Margaret's father Edward and her mother Agatha formed a small ex-patriate Saxon community in the village of Mecseknadasd in south-west Hungary. Alan Wilson observes:

There is, in that small and isolated German-speaking village in the south of Hungary, an overwhelming interest in the Scottish saint. There is also a humbling welcome for those who come to seek out information about a young girl and her family who lived in the area for little more than a decade almost a thousand years ago.

Lifting the veil of a thousand years, Alan Wilson favours Saxon rather than Hungarian descent in the Scottish queen's family tree. The colourful saga of Margaret's father's flight from his native England and eventual arrival at the hospitable court of Hungary, via Scandinavia and Kiev, throws light on the interaction of European dynasties a thousand years ago. Whether she was Hungarian by blood or not, however, Margaret was deeply moulded by her upbringing in that newly converted country on the fringes of European Christendom.

Seeking to link his country more strongly with the Christian West, King Stephen of Hungary (crowned on the first Christmas Day of the first new millennium after Christ) had been anxious to eradicate traces of Eastern Orthodoxy as well as to put down paganism. He did so with great cruelty, but Stephen has an enduring place in the hearts of Hungarian people. In 1999, on the tenth anniversary of the collapse of the Berlin wall, a Hungarian train driver told a Scots journalist, 'It was such a feeling we had when Hungary became a free and independent state, just as it was founded by Saint Stephen.'[29]

Cruelly though King Stephen of Hungary dealt with dissidents, he nevertheless put forward a strong plea for tolerance and a pluralist society which Europe is barely beginning to achieve a thousand years later. 'For as guests arrive from different parts or provinces, so do they bring with them different values and customs, different weaponry and sciences, and all this adorns the country… For a country of one language and one culture is weak and fallible,' the King instructed his son. 'Therefore I enjoin on you, my son, to protect newcomers benevolently and to hold them in high esteem, so that they should stay with you rather than dwell elsewhere.'[30]

MARGARET BECOMES QUEEN OF SCOTLAND, 1070

Are not two sparrows sold for a penny? Yet not one of them will fall to the ground apart from the will of your Father. (Matthew 10:29)

When Margaret was ten, her father, with strong claims to the English throne, returned to England with his family. He died in unknown circumstances soon afterwards. The arrival of William of Normandy in 1066 forced Margaret's mother, Agatha, to flee from London with Margaret, her sister Christina and her brother Edgar and to seek asylum from Malcolm III, *Ceann Mor* ('great chief' or 'head') of Scotland. He had earlier sought refuge himself at the Saxon court, fleeing from the murderous Macbeth, and, as the *Anglo-Saxon Chronicle* puts it, he 'began to yearn for [Edgar's] sister Margaret as his wife'. But Margaret's aspirations were set on the cloister and she refused Malcolm's advances. The Chronicle continues: 'The King eagerly urged her brother until he said "yea" to it, and indeed he dared not do otherwise, even as He Himself saith in His gospel that even a sparrow cannot fall into a snare without His design.'[31]

However, Margaret was no sparrow and Malcolm III of Scotland was no barbarian ogre. The King of Scots was fluent in Norman French, his own native Gaelic and Saxon English, and doubtless had a knowledge of Lowland Scots. Malcolm and Margaret were to point their country towards the continent of Europe—but, as mentioned in Chapter 1, divisions were becoming more sharply focused within Scotland between the Gaelic-speaking north and the Scots-speaking Lothians. By marrying a non-Gaelic-speaking queen, as well as by his dealings with the Norman court south of the Border, which would eventually cost him his life, Malcolm widened the rift within the ancient kingdom of Alba.

But when 24-year-old Margaret married 40-year-old Malcolm in his capital city, Dunfermline, in 1070, the *Anglo-Saxon Chronicle* and other historians of the time lauded the match. 'For she was to increase God's praise in the land, and to direct the king from his erring way, and his people with him; and to suppress the evil customs which that people had formerly used.'[32]

This is an overstatement. Just as the Victorians talked about 'darkest Africa' to emphasize the virtues of their own civilization, Malcolm had to be portrayed as errant and his people barbarous in order to point up the right practices of his queen. Margaret reorganized Scottish religious observance, bringing such practices as the keeping of Ash Wednesday into line with mainstream European Christendom. She also introduced monastic communities to Scotland, especially the Benedictines. Criticized for anglicizing Scotland and for blocking what are seen as the pure springs of Celtic spirituality by her Romish ways, Margaret in fact repaired a ragged patchwork. She emphasized Christian values in the court; and she and her royal husband—not hitherto known as merciful—'waited upon Christ in the person of His poor', as her biographer Bishop Turgot puts it. Turgot also describes her care of 'nine orphan little children, who were utterly destitute':

For she ordered soft food, such as little children delight in, to be prepared for them daily; and when the little ones were brought to her, she did not think it beneath her to take them on her knee and make little sups for them, and to place them in their mouths with the spoons she herself used.[33]

Edinburgh-born Robert Louis Stevenson has written, 'It is the history of our kindness that alone makes this world tolerable.'[34] In a cruel age, Margaret brought to her adopted land compassion and kindness, a legacy for which she is remembered even after a thousand years.

MEDIEVAL SCOTLAND: MAKARS AND MONARCHS

You heavens above, rain down righteousness; let clouds shower it down. (Isaiah 45:8).

Three of Margaret's sons reigned after her. Edgar (the first king of Scots to have a Saxon name) and his brother Alexander both died childless. Margaret's youngest son, David (also an untypical name for Scotland, perhaps linking him with the court of Hungary), became king in 1124.

Alexander and David continued to bring religious orders from the Continent to Scotland. Indeed, David founded so many abbeys and churches (including Holyrood) that he has been nicknamed 'The Sair [costly] Sanct'—for the nation had to bear the cost. A poet writing in Gaelic also seems to have disliked the king, who had been brought up south of the Border:

> It's bad, what Mael Coluim's son has done,
>   dividing us from Alexander;
> he causes, like each king's son before,
>   the plunder of stable Alba.[35]

However, Scotland enjoyed peace and prosperity under David. Town life flourished; David developed royal burghs, and a main street in Edinburgh's Old Town, the Canongate, is linked with him: the canons from Holyrood Abbey would walk along the Canongate, perhaps bearing corn to grind at Canonmills, now part of Stockbridge. ('Gate' comes from the Scandinavian word for 'street'.)

A legend connected with the founding of Holyrood ('rood' means 'cross') says that King David once went out with his horses and hounds to hunt. He came upon a white stag and eagerly notched an arrow in his bow. But the stag was no ordinary beast—in the old pagan traditions, white was the colour for immortality. The stag spoke to David, asking the king to stay his hand, and then David noticed a golden cross between the white stag's antlers. He fell to his knees. The abbey (taken apart stone by stone after James VII, the last reigning Stewart king, was banished in 1688) was built on the spot where David had met the stag. The palace grew up beside it as a residence for royal pilgrims.

The church reforms and innovation by Margaret, her sons and grandsons produced a network of about a thousand tithe-funded parishes organized into twelve dioceses. Within the structures of the medieval Scottish Church were also great religious houses, hospitals, collegiate churches and private chapels.

CHRISTIAN ART AND POETRY OF MEDIEVAL SCOTLAND

My heart is stirred by a noble theme as I recite my verses for the king; my tongue is the pen of a skilful writer. (Psalm 45:1)

Fourteenth-century England produced great Christian mystics. Medieval Scotland, however, has left a legacy of stone-carving, of illustrated psalters and breviaries and a poetry whose greatness is undiminished by time—as well as clarion calls for freedom. The breviaries show that the old Celtic saints who had been elbowed out by the religious orders were still honoured, as we have seen with Triduana. Indeed, the happy interchange of saints of both traditions, Celtic and Roman Catholic, would be kept up until the Reformation. For example, during a time of plague in England in 1379, the Scots reivers (raiders) kept up their raids across the Border and, believing that the plague had been sent by God upon England for its repentance, prayed for deliverance: 'God and Saint Mungo, Saint Romayne and Saint Andrew shield us this day from the foul death that Englishmen died upon.'[36]

This book can only give a brief overview of the whole period, a rough chart to an abundant treasure trove.

The liturgical music of medieval Scotland fell out of favour during the Reformation. It was felt that such music was for 'carnal not spiritual minds' and was 'unbiblical and unsupported by sound tradition'.[37] However, this type of sacred music is now being recovered and sung again. One such piece—the *Sprouston Breviary*—is associated with Kentigern or Mungo (d. 612), the patron saint of Glaschu, or Glasgow, 'the dear green place' which grew up around the church founded by Mungo and dedicated to him. The city's coat of arms shows the saint wearing a bishop's mitre above a motto: 'Let Glasgow flourish...'. (The motto in full continues: '...by the preaching of the Lord and the teaching of his Word'.) Around the saint are the symbols of his legend—a fish with a ring in its mouth, a bell, a bird and a tree.

The fish, the ring and the bird feature in the saint's life as told in the *Sprouston Breviary*. Dated around 1300, this Latin rhymed liturgy for the feast of St Kentigern is based on sources which go back to the seventh century. The music for its magnificent collection of readings and responses was uncovered by John Purser in his researches for a BBC Radio Scotland series, 'Scotland's Music', and was performed by *Cappella Nova* in 1997 for the first time in 700 years.

A Renaissance composer of great talent, Robert Carver (c.1490–c.1546), is also at last finding his place in Scottish music after a silence of more than 400 years. Carver was an Augustinian monk at Cambuskenneth, a monastery close to Stirling and therefore with close links with the Scottish court. Only one manuscript survives but it shows that the Scottish medieval church could reach heights comparable with the most distinguished European composers; indeed, one piece which includes a *cantus firmus* (main tune) called *L'homme armé* is the only British example of its kind, although the form was used often on the Continent, notably by Palestrina. Robert Carver's Masses and motets are composed on a big scale—probably therefore designed for the lofty setting of a Chapel Royal. Happily, Carver's rich music is being performed and recorded today and is finding the audience it deserves.[38]

The Scottish kings and the clan chiefs of Gaelic Scotland alike were generous patrons of composers and musicians. Gaelic music—particularly for the *clarsach*, the small, portable harp—showed a remarkable readiness to experiment and innovate. Indeed, there seems to have been a marked revival of religious life in Argyll and the Isles during the 16th century—in other words, a regeneration which stood in clear contrast to the decay in southern Scotland at the time of the Reformation.[39]

Another collection of manuscripts from the period, *The Book of the Dean of Lismore*, has survived. It contains poems in praise of God and the chief, heroic ballads, love songs and laments. A 15th-century elegy may show an example of the virtues admired by the society which produced it—'hospitable and generous'—and of a poetry which, even in translation, has power, tenderness and immediacy:

O rosary that has awakened my tear, dear the finger that was wont to be on thee; dear the heart, hospitable and generous, which owned thee ever until tonight. Sad am I for his death, he whose hand thou didst each hour encircle... Mary Mother, who did nurse the King, may she guard me on every path, and her Son, who created each creature, O rosary that has awakened my tear.[40]

Much of the early music and poetry has been lost, but what is left is of outstanding craftsmanship and attests a culture of wealth and vigour.

WEST HIGHLAND MEDIEVAL STONE CROSSES

Deliver my life from the sword, my precious life from the power of the dogs. (Psalm 22:20)

The medieval era also saw a remarkable development of West Highland stone-carving, much of it with explicitly Christian themes. The principal schools of stone-carving included Kintyre, Iona, Oronsay, Keills and Loch Awe—but the stone-carvers received commissions far beyond Argyll. This outstanding monumental sculpture speaks of a vital ecclesiastical heritage and a powerful aristocracy. Richly carved free-standing crosses, found nowhere else in Britain at this period, have since suffered the vicissitudes of weather and religious attack. One of these fine crosses, until very recently, stood outside the parish church of Kilmartin in Mid-Argyll. Noble even in adversity, the young Christ had hung mutilated on his broken cross since the Reformation, both arms lopped off, his bowed head devoid of its halo. Only towards the end of the 20th century did researchers discover two broken pieces and part of the missing halo, which have now been replaced. An angel surmounts the Crucified King, whose majesty is apparent even in this ruined state. The cross, now much visited, has been brought into the parish church, along with other fragments from the Loch Awe school of stone-carvers, including an intricately carved eighth-century cross-slab.

About fifteen miles away, in Knapdale beyond Loch Sween, the thickset walls of ruined Kilmory Chapel (the church of Mary) houses a similar rich collection of crosses and memorial stones. Here, amidst carved graveslabs and humbler quern-stones for the grinding of grain, is a magnificent mid-15th-century cross, nearly three metres high. For centuries this beautiful cross stood intact and scarcely weathered outside the chapel on a windy headland facing the Isle of Jura. Now the cross has been taken into the little museum. Called the Macmillan cross, it was probably commissioned by a chief of that name. A rich border of interlace encircles the Christ, whose hands, poignantly large in proportion to his frame, are firmly nailed in stone. Two figures attend him—the Virgin Mary and the apostle John. A lion-like beast crouches on the right, and the interlace leads down the shaft of the cross to a plaited border and a sword, its hilt uppermost. On the reverse side of the cross, interlace terminates in the tail of a snarling hound whose teeth are about to plunge into the neck of an antlered deer. Two more dogs pursue the hunted stag and, with hue and cry, the hooded huntsman brings up the rear of this remarkable hunting scene. His feet are firmly planted on the interlace at the foot of the cross. His cudgel is raised towards his dogs and their prey, and a huge hunting-horn is slung around his waist. His tunic falls in pronounced folds about his knees.

Does the powerful scene represent Psalm 22:20: 'Deliver my life from the sword, my precious life from the power of the dogs'? Is Christ, the warrior-hero, being likened to a deer brought to bay? Would a Highland stone-carver in medieval Scotland have known the Bible? Wasn't the great cry of the Reformers that the Bible 'suld be preichit fra towne to towne' ('should be preached from town to town')?[41]

Yes, the Reformers rightly clamoured for the Bible to be translated out of Latin into 'our tongue Vulgare', as the playwright Sir David Lyndsay put it in his drama *Ane Pleasant Satyre of the Thrie Estatis*. But in the medieval period, although few people possessed books, which were exorbitantly expensive, and many clergy were poorly educated in Latin, the Bible was woven inextricably into the life and consciousness of people. The Passion of Christ, together with the whole biblical drama from Adam and Eve to the Last Judgment, was performed in street theatre throughout Christendom. In Dundee in 1505, props included a cradle and three babies made of cloth ('a credil and thre barnis maid of clath'), while fifteen years later the actor who played Christ required a leather coat with stockings and gloves ('cristis cott of lethyr with the hoss and glufis').[42]

Every church was its own visual aid, with the whole Bible drama depicted in paint, on glass and in wood and stone carving. The liturgy of the Church (sung in Latin) provided its own commentary on biblical texts, including the Apocrypha. So while it is true that very few people possessed even a portion of scripture, and certainly not in their own native speech, the people of medieval Scotland were perhaps better versed in scripture (interpreted by tradition) than is generally the case today.

This shows in the work of the poets and storytellers—and not only in their devotional work. Satire and fable were shaped by scripture—for example, in the animal fables of a major poet and storyteller of the 15th century, Robert Henryson. Henryson was a master of style, pawky and humorous, bitingly satirical. He was steeped in the classics (his 'Troilus and Cressyd' is intricately wrought), and deeply Christian: his poem 'The Bludy Serk' ('The Bloody Shirt') uses features of conventional romance to develop the story of the fall, redemption and the Passion of the Lord. It shows how closely woven into the culture of the day was the story of the salvation of humankind.

SURREXIT DOMINUS DE SEPULCHRO: THE POETRY OF WILLIAM DUNBAR

But Christ has indeed been raised from the dead, the firstfruits of those who have fallen asleep. (1 Corinthians 15:20)

The greatest poet of medieval Scotland was the Franciscan friar, court poet and chaplain, William Dunbar (c. 1460–1515). In a poem which begins 'Done is the battell on the dragon blak...', Dunbar welcomes the resurrection with a shout of triumph which resounds like a Bach toccata. He also hymns the incarnation with tenderness and hope. This poem can be found set to music in *The Oxford Book of Carols*.

Dunbar writes in a splendidly subtle and malleable Scots which he can make gentle and melodious, bawdy or riotous to suit his themes. He often uses a Latin refrain, but in one of the greatest poems ever written on

Christ's Passion the refrain, 'O mankynd, for the luif of thee' ('O mankind, for thy love'), alternates half-way through the poem with 'Thy blissit salvatour Jesu' ('Thy blessed Saviour, Jesus'). Both are in poignant, lyrical Scots. The poem is set on the eve of Easter and begins with a dream motif, which takes us back to 'The Dream of the Rood', for in his sleep the poet witnesses the Passion.

Dunbar's poem also evokes the narrow lanes of Edinburgh, along which many a thief would have been dragged, bound with ropes, to punishment. The punishment of Christ continues relentlessly—and the language exactly fits the pain. It is reminiscent of the Anglo-Saxon poem, of the writings of Lady Julian of Norwich, and also of the annual performance of medieval street theatre. The mystery plays had made the Passion of Christ as familiar to the most illiterate child as the events of the latest TV soap are to us today. But, writing within the tradition, Dunbar transcends it—and once again the music of Bach comes to mind in the melody of the words, not least the poignant reference to the nakedness of Christ—'and him all nakit on the tree':

> On to the cross of breadth and length
> They stretched him out with all their strength,
> While on the rood as on a rack
> They fastened him with iron tacks,
> And him all naked on the tree
> They raised him high for all to see.[43]

Under Dunbar the poetry of Scotland, secular and Christian, reached heights which were not to be achieved again, not even by Burns, until a poet from Langholm, just across the Border, changed his name from C.M. Grieve to Hugh MacDiarmid (1892–1978) and carved out of Lallans (Lowland Scots) a language which has set Scottish literature on to a new, confident course. The challenge to the churches, as we shall see in Chapter 10, is to keep up with the pace in a new Scotland increasingly at ease with its own identity.

'AH, FREEDOM IS A NOBLE THING!'

If the Son makes you free, you will be free indeed. (John 8:32)

The Middle Ages in Scotland saw Scotland fight for independence within a Christian Europe. National strivings, holy relics (such as the Breac-bennoch of Columba) and calls for freedom have shaped the consciousness of the Scottish nation. Writing in 1450, about 'Braveheart' William Wallace's struggle for freedom 150 years before, Walter Bower, Abbot of Inchcolm (the Island of Columba) in the Forth, quotes the warlord as saying: 'When I was growing up, I learned from my uncle, a priest, to value this one proverb above all riches, and I have always held it in my mind: This is the truth I tell you: of all things freedom's most fine.'[44]

These words, 'of all things freedom's most fine', echo the opening of a great epic written around 1360 by John Barbour, the Archdeacon of Aberdeen: 'Ah! Freedom is a noble thing!'

It was in the cause of freedom that William Wallace went to Glasgow to see Bishop Robert Wishart, an ardent patriot and a fiery leader in the revolt against Edward I. Wallace was betrayed on 5 August 1305, in a house in Robroyston, approximately five miles north-east of the medieval city. A 30-foot stone cross with a sword above a Scots lion rampant (standing erect) was put up in 1900 to mark the spot. Wallace was taken south in chains, humiliated and cruelly executed. He has never been forgotten, and Walter Bower was only the first of a long line of authors to write about the Scottish patriot who laid down his life for freedom, forging Scots national consciousness in the fires of his self-sacrifice.

Freedom was finally won at the Battle of Bannockburn in 1314 by the Gaelic-speaking descendant of a Norman family from Picardy, Robert the Bruce, but struggles with the nation south of the Border continued until James VI became king of both Scotland and England in 1603.

The Church was at the centre of medieval national striving. The long-drawn-out struggle for national identity sometimes known as the Wars of Independence lasted more than a hundred years, from 1296 to 1424, when James I of Scotland was freed from captivity in England and came north with his bride, Lady Joan Beaufort. The struggle against England then became more like a cold war which has marked the Scottish psyche to this day, but the conflict was not about the glorification of the monarchy or the privileges of noble caste, but about liberty and human dignity understood in a Christian way with 'the due consent and assent of us all', as the Declaration of Arbroath put it. This most famous Scottish statement of freedom, much quoted today, was written in Latin in 1320 in the Abbey of Arbroath by the Abbot, Bernard of Linton, Chancellor of Scotland, and sealed by eight earls and 31 barons. It is important to note that the Declaration was addressed to the Pope. This is significant because it shows that in the medieval period Scotland was firmly linked into an as-yet-undivided European entity. The Declaration of Arbroath, born of this awareness of the nation's place in a larger European community, contains words of enduring importance: 'For we fight, not for glory, nor riches, nor for honour, but only and alone for freedom, which no good man surrenders but with his life.' This Declaration, one of the key documents of Scottish history, also contains an important sentence clearly differentiating Scotland from England and acknowledging 'the gentle Andrew' as patron saint:

Their (the Scots) true nobility and merits have been made plain (the nobility of Scotland informs the Pope) if by no other considerations, then by the fact that the King of Kings, the Lord Jesus Christ, after his passion and resurrection, brought them, the first of all, to his holy faith, though they lived in the furthest parts of the world, and he chose that they be so persuaded to faith by none other than the brother of the blessed Peter, the gentle Andrew, first called of the apostles... whom he wished always to be over us as our patron.[45]

With such credentials, then, medieval Scotland proudly claimed its place in Christian Europe.

CHAPTER 5

THE REFORMATION

'Din and Play in Our Kirk'

**I will make boys their officials; mere children will
govern them... Youths oppress my people, women rule
over them. O, my people, your guides lead you astray;
they turn you from the path.**

ISAIAH 3:4, 12

By the 16th century, new nation states were emerging in Europe. Old
certainties were questioned as explorers pushed back the boundaries of
the known world. Printing made books—and not least the Bible—more
widely available. And in Scotland, too, voices clamoured for change.

The text from Isaiah, 'youths oppress my people', seemed especially
relevant in Scotland when illegitimate infant sons of the nobility were
made abbots or bishops. And when, following the death of James V in
1542, Scotland was ruled first by Mary of Guise, mother of Mary Queen
of Scots, and then by her daughter, voices complained that the third
chapter of the prophet Isaiah had been fulfilled in an afflicted nation.

There was a hunger for a simple evangelical faith and for the Bible to
be available in a language people could understand. Although some

higher clergy actively worked for reform, many resisted popular demand. It was felt that translation from Latin into the vernacular would cheapen the precious mystery of Holy Writ. A talented young theologian, 24-year-old Patrick Hamilton, was publicly burnt to death in 1528 for demanding that people should be able to read the Bible in their own tongue. Patrick Hamilton's death has gone down in Scottish Presbyterian history as the starting point of the Reformation (I can remember drawing the grisly scene for a history homework exercise); and it is likely that loyal Catholics found it distasteful too. None the less, an Act of Parliament in 1536 banned all versions of the Bible except the Latin. Among those condemned as a result of this Act was Thomas Forret, vicar of Dollar, who had the audacity to quote scripture in English and to carry a copy of the Bible in English about with him—in his sleeve. Here is an extract from his trial:

Accuser: *Thou false heretic! Thou learned (taught) all thy parishoners to say the Paternoster, the Creed and the Ten Commandments in English, which is contrary to our acts that they should know what they say.*

Forret: *Brother, my people are so rude and ignorant they understand no Latin…*
The apostle Paul says in his doctrin to the Corinthians that he had rather speak five words to the understanding and edifying of his people, than ten thousand in a strange tongue which they understand not.

Accuser: *Where finds thou that?*

Forret: *In my books, here in my sleeve.*

Accuser (grabbing the book): *Behold, sirs, he has the book of Heresy in his sleeve, that makes all the din and play in our Kirk!*

Forret: *God forgive you! You could say better, if you pleased, nor to call the book of the Evangel of Jesus Christ the book of Heresy!*

Accuser: *Knowest thou not, heretic, that it is contrary to our acts and express commands, to have a New Testament or Bible in English, which is enough to burn thee for?*

Then the Council of the Clergy gave sentence on him to be burnt, for the using of the same book—the New Testament in Inglis (English).[46]

Forret was burnt in Edinburgh in 1539.

Newly discovered truths of scripture were propagated by drama and verse. Sir David Lyndsay, chief poet at the court of James V (1513–42), wrote *Ane Pleasant Satyre of the Thrie Estaitis*. Reprinted in Edinburgh in 1568 and 1599, the play pleads on behalf of common people who are duped by false clergy while the precious pearl of Holy Scripture is withheld. Performed as Scotland's contribution to the first International Edinburgh Festival in 1946, Lyndsay's play has had many repeat perform-ances, including a highly successful tour of Poland in the 1980s. In its own day the play was a plea for reform, but also for tolerance.

Sixteenth-century Scotland produced a song which is still sung today. It comes from the Wedderburn brothers' *Gude and Godlie Ballads*, and in its turn derives from Luther's carol, *Von Himmel Hoch*. It is a lullaby to Christ entitled 'Balulalow'. This intimate expression of devotion is a sign that people were attuned to a personal faith, rather than looking to major changes in church structures. The monasteries were not in themselves corrupt; the problem lay with finances. Henry VIII's 'Rough Wooing' had brought a trail of costly devastation. Trade had been badly affected. The collegiate churches of Scotland, together with the three University Colleges—Glasgow (founded in 1453), Aberdeen (1495), and St Andrews (1512, 1544)—all needed money. Monasteries, which were property-owning institutions, had also been affected by a slump in the wool trade. Parishes had therefore been bled for their revenues, and humble lay people were the hardest hit. The chief complaint of the poor was the unfair weight of tithes and rents which they had to pay the parish. The parish clergy were often ignorant and avaricious. A poem of the period complains that the curate cares more about the fines he pockets for non-attendance at Easter services than about the spiritual needs of his flock:

> *His thought is more upon the pasch [Easter] fines*
> *Than the souls in purgatory that pines.*[47]

The impetus for Reformation grew among urban working families, notably in Perth where five men and a woman, Helen Stark, were executed on 25 January 1544 for supporting the new doctrines. Helen Stark's husband (James Ronaldson, a skinner) was hanged with the other four men—

William Anderson, maltman; James Hunter, flesher (butcher); James Finlayson, labourer; and Robert Lamb, merchant. Helen Stark, a mother of four, asked to be allowed to die with her husband, but her sentence was to drown. She was allowed to accompany him to the foot of the scaffold. 'Husband, rejoice,' she said, 'for we have lived together many joyful days; but this day in which we must die ought to be most joyful to us both, because we must have joy for ever. Therefore I will not bid you goodnight, for we shall suddenly meet with joy in the kingdom of heaven.' After the men were hanged, Helen Stark was escorted to South Inch, where she was tied in a weighted sack and drowned, leaving a newborn baby and three other children.[48]

The deaths of these five, as well as Patrick Hamilton and eight others, were the responsibility of Cardinal Beaton of St Andrews, who quickly became demonized as the archetypal Catholic enemy of Reformation, a 'bloody butcher', a tyrant and a womaniser. The Cardinal was murdered in 1546.

JOHN KNOX, 'A PAINFUL PREACHER OF THE BLESSED EVANGEL'

The Lord commanded us to obey all these decrees and to fear the Lord our God, so that we might always prosper and be kept alive, as is the case today. And if we are careful to obey all this law before the Lord our God, as he has commanded us, that will be our righteousness. (Deuteronomy 6:24–25)

Educated at the University of St Andrews, John Knox (c.1512–72) had been ordained as a priest. Cardinal Beaton's extreme treatment of Protestant activists pushed Knox, who had already espoused reform, from the Roman Catholic Church. He became chaplain to Beaton's assassins: the Commandment 'You must not kill' (Exodus 20:13) was flexibly interpreted by both sides in the struggle for doctrinal rectitude and church supremacy. Knox was arrested, spent two years as a galley slave of the French, and thereafter studied in Geneva, steeping himself in the doctrines of John Calvin which he brought back to Scotland. His return proved to be the catalyst for radical changes.

Knox addressed his new theology not just to individuals, but to the nation as a whole, speaking at grassroots level.

For considering myself rather called of God to instruct the ignorant, comfort the sorrowful, confirm the weak, and rebuke the proud, by tongue and lively voice in these corrupt days, than to compose books for the age to come, seeing so much is written… and yet so little well observed… it hath pleased his mercy to make me not a lord-like Bishop but a painful Preacher of the blessed Evangel.[49]

Knox held a high view of the supremacy of scripture which was to influence the Scottish Kirk profoundly. Here he is, replying to his Sovereign, Mary, who wondered how to choose between differing interpretations of scripture:

Ye shall believe God, that plainly speaketh in his word: and further than the word teaches you, ye shall neither believe the ane or the other. The word of God is plain in the self (itself); and if there appear any obscurity in one place, the Holy Ghost… explains the same more clearly in other places.[50]

Knox's response clearly left no room for discussion, but Mary had her own ideas. Her poems on sacred themes reflect her trust in her 'Seigneur et Pere Souverain' and the following verse, stressing the value of penitence, may be a poetic reply to John Knox:

Mais qui poura, O Pere, tres humanin,
Avoir cet heur, si tu n'y mets la main
D'abondonner son peche et offense
En ayant fait condigne penitence?

(But which of us, O kindest Father, still
Can claim this fortune, save it be thy will
That he abandon sin and all offence
By having made a worthy penitence?)[51]

Knox's preaching had made a strong impact on some notable lords of Scotland, including the Duke of Argyll, chief of Clan Campbell, whose family would defend the Protestant position through the troubled years of the next century. The immediate upshot of this was that an Act of Parliament in August 1560 made Scotland officially Protestant and outlawed the Roman Catholic Church. This parliament was well attended but the proceedings which led to the passing of the Act were far from being cut and dried: many clergy kept their previous charges and revenues. Although the Mass was now abolished (as was jurisdiction by the Pope), and a Protestant Confession of Faith had been accepted, things on the religious front remained rather ambiguous—and were even more so when Mary returned from France the following year. The queen continued to observe Catholic practice, which meant that courtiers and servants and even townspeople attended worship which was officially illegal. However, it is the opinion of a present-day Catholic historian, Father Mark Dilworth, that 'Catholic resistance to the Reformation was feeble, sporadic and uncoordinated. It looks as if Catholics simply lacked the will to win and there was no leadership'.[52]

If the Roman Catholic clerical wing of the 'thrie estaitis' was lacking in will and leadership, the lords temporal looked to their own self-interest and welcomed new warmth in relationships with Protestant England. They hoped for a strong voice in the new Reformed Church. The burgesses who formed the backbone of trade and commerce also looked to closer ties with England. The poor and disadvantaged, however, saw the reforms as an attack on the rich and privileged. Bands of vagrants and beggars were not found wanting in helping to dismantle ecclesiastical centres which had prospered at their expense. But by and large the old holy places simply became redundant and were left to crumble, their stones appropriated for local needs, since the Reformers taught that no place should be considered sacred. John Knox stated unequivocally:

Our Master Christ Jesus appointed us to no one certain place where we shall be assured of his presence, but rather forbidding the observation of all places, he sends us his own spiritual presence, saying, 'Wheresoever two or three are gathered in my name, there am I in the midst of them.'[53]

'Forbidding the observation of all places…'. The consequence of this teaching is that if the place is not the focus of worship, neither is the keeper of the place, the priest. The seeds were being sown for a radical change in which every believer would have the right to read and interpret Scripture. Nevertheless, Christian pluralism was driven out of Scotland on the heels of the deposed Queen Mary, who fled her kingdom in 1567, having given her throne to her infant son whom she never saw again. From now on, Scotland was on course to consolidate the Presbyterian form of the Protestant faith. Although the first Assembly of 1560 had sworn allegiance to the queen, the new wave of reform had to justify its rebellion against the monarch. The atmosphere was highly charged when the General Assembly met in Edinburgh in 1567, following the enforced departure of the queen. This Assembly was more cohesive than that of 1560 and also more avowedly Calvinist. It had no new programme but aimed to build on the foundation already laid. Even so, progress was by no means uniform throughout the country.

Mary herself misguidedly sought succour from her cousin, Elizabeth Tudor. The English queen kept her Scottish cousin in prison for 19 years. Mary, dowager queen of France, heiress to the English throne, had arguably a stronger claim to the Crown than Elizabeth herself, and she became the focus of diplomatic intrigue and domestic plots to dethrone Elizabeth. Her execution was one of political expediency, neither the first nor the last of the age. Almost her last words were for her son, James: 'Commend me to my son, and tell him that I have not done anything that may prejudice his kingdom of Scotland,' she said.

Letters she had written to James over the years, and gifts she made him, were mostly withheld from him. When Elizabeth signed his mother's death warrant, the king of Scotland did not protest.

Although baptized Catholic, Mary's son James had little choice but to be Protestant—and was soundly instructed in Reformation theology. One of the Reformers, Andrew Melville, called the king 'God's sillie (simple) vassal' and told the young monarch bluntly: 'I mon tell yow, thair is twa Kings and twa kingdomes in Scotland. Thair is Chryst Jesus the King, and his kingdome is the Kirk, whose subject King James the Saxt is, and of whase kingdome nocht a king nor a lord nor a heid, bot a member.'

('I must tell you there are two kings and two kingdoms in Scotland. There is Christ Jesus the king, and his kingdom is the Church whose subject King James the Sixth is, and of whose kingdom not a king nor a lord nor a head, but a member.')

This radical talk was not at all to the king's liking; and once he was made king of England as well as Scotland in 1603, James quickly showed his preference for Anglicanism—not least because the monarch was supreme earthly governor of the church south of the Border. James tried to restore bishops to the Presbyterian Church and directly attacked the very spirit of the Scottish Reformation. James' son, Charles I, betrayed his total ignorance of the mood of his northern kingdom by foolishly appointing the 1637 Scottish Prayer Book for use throughout Scotland.

The story goes that when the king's clergyman, robed in Anglican vestments, stood forward in the High Kirk of St Giles in Edinburgh on 23 July 1637 to read from the new Prayer Book, a local woman, Jenny Geddes, vented her disapproval. In those days there were still no pews in church (medieval cathedrals had stone ledges around the walls, hence the saying 'the weakest go to the wall'). But come the Reformation, as sermons got longer, a little stool became part of people's churchgoing equipment. Jenny Geddes is reputed to have hurled hers at the minister, crying, 'Dinnae say mass at my lug' ('Don't say Mass in my ear').

In any event, the service was broken up, a mob stormed St Giles and the dean and the bishop were hustled out. However, Charles remained inflexible in the face of growing opposition to his policies and the National Covenant was signed on 1 March 1638 in Greyfriars Kirk—the first post-Reformation church to be built in Edinburgh. Some of the most powerful nobles and gentry of Scotland signed the Covenant; many, it is said, dipped the pen into their own blood.

The National Covenant (which opposed bishops and prayers printed in set forms and read from books) was a lengthy and far from revolutionary document but it forced Charles to take notice of the dissent north of the Border, not least because many of the noblemen who signed were allegedly his men. The signing of the National Covenant, however, was followed by a secret Assembly which met behind locked doors in Glasgow Cathedral. This Assembly was attended by ministers of the Kirk and—for the first time ever—all Scotland's 63 presbyteries. This was people power, however much it was filtered through the hierarchies of the Church. It was also a rebel Assembly which uncompromisingly affirmed not only that Scotland was Presbyterian, in defiance of the stated wish of the king, but that the whole of Britain should become so as well. Scotland was now on course for confrontation with the government in Westminster. Many heads would roll, including the king's, in January 1649. The Glasgow Assembly led directly to armed conflict in 1639 and to the signing of the Solemn League and Covenant in 1643, a more radical document which looked to the overthrow of episcopacy within the setting of a close union of Christian (Presbyterian) government in both Scotland and England.

However, by no means all the signatories of the first Covenant supported the claims of the second. Many of the noble signatories of the National Covenant now drew back from what was becoming an increasingly rebellious stance against the king. A notable abstainer was James Graham, the Marquis of Montrose. Montrose conducted a brilliant military campaign on behalf of the Crown from 1644 to 1645. His support was strongest in the Gaelic-speaking west, where a number of Catholic priests joined his army as chaplains—as did an Irish Catholic force under the command of Alasdair MacColla, a brilliant general who led 2000 men and Montrose's own handful to one victory after another. Covenanting armies were routed, and although, by and large, civilians were spared, Montrose had on his conscience the sack of Aberdeen in 1644, a three-day rampage of looting and murder which fuelled Protestant prejudice against the Catholic Irish.

Montrose, who was an essentially honourable man, faithful to his king and to his wife, as well as being a talented military leader, was finally defeated and ignominiously executed in Edinburgh on 21 August 1650. Dressed in scarlet, in silk stockings and fine linen, he was transported in an open cart from the Tolbooth Prison up the High Street to the gallows. It is said that his enemies had gathered to jeer but fell silent; and 'the hangman wept as he pushed him off,' writes one of the Marquis's best-known biographers, John Buchan.[54]

Montrose was 'pushed off' to a terrible death: to be hung for three hours and then to be beheaded and quartered, his limbs to be put on public display. The marquis gave his hangman a gold coin and went to his gruesome death eighteen months after the execution of the king in whose cause he died. After the Restoration in 1660, on the orders of Charles II, the dismembered remains of Montrose were given a state funeral in St Giles. A new royalist epoch had begun which boded ill for the staunchest followers of Scotland's Solemn League and Covenant.

'BROTHER, DIE WELL, IT IS THE LAST ACT OF FAITH YOU WILL EVER BE ABLE TO DO': THE 'KILLING TIME'

They will put you out of the synagogue; in fact, a time is coming when anyone who kills you will think he is offering a service to God. (John 16:2)

After the signing to the Solemn League and Covenant, Scots were legally at war on three fronts: against Royalist England, against the forces of Papacy and Episcopacy in Ireland and against those in the Gaelic-speaking Highlands.

None the less, although the Covenanters saw Charles I as Anti-Christ, who deserved to be deposed and executed (1649), they did not want war but peace on their terms. They supported the cause of Charles II, hoping that he would honour their cause in return. It was not to be. Despite royal promises to the contrary, Charles II imposed Episcopalian curates of questionable character in the Scottish churches and outlawed dissident ministers. Dissent was particularly strong in southern and western Scotland. In the parish of Anwoth, in Kirkudbright, lived one of Scotland's greatest theologians, Samuel Rutherford (1600–61). Loyal to the Covenant until his death, Rutherford won international fame and turned down offers of professorships in Holland and Utrecht. He thrashed out a theology that had direct bearing on the political arguments of the day. He denied the divine right of kings and argued that the monarch was chosen by the will of the people, who were at liberty to resist a tyrant. Rutherford was banned from ministry and exiled to Aberdeen, where he wrote over 300 letters to his spiritual children, who were to be found in every rank of society—peasant farmers and lawyers, noble ladies, ministers and ploughmen. Still reprinted and widely read today, Samuel Rutherford's letters and sermons were eagerly received in parishes over Scotland, fuelling the zeal for the Covenant, for which he suffered the pain of seeing his writings burned by the public hangman. When Charles II visited Scotland, Rutherford boldly informed the monarch that the duty of kings was to obey Christ and honour the Solemn League and Covenant. As a result he was cited to appear before Parliament. But Rutherford knew that he was dying. He replied, 'I have got summons already before a Superior Judge and Judicatory, and I behove to answer my first summons, and ere your day come I will be where few kings and great folks come.'[55]

The price of non-conformity to the Episcopal Church imposed by the king was high. A new Act of Parliament in 1661 evicted dissenting Presbyterian ministers from their parishes. And to make sure that no one in the parish harboured or helped them, soldiers were quartered in villages and towns. People were fined if they absented themselves from Sunday services led by the hated curates. Peasant farmers, who subsisted on the verge of destitution at best of times, were forced to feed soldiers who ate whole families literally out of house and home—and then, out of spite, took away their Bibles, their greatcoats and plaids, so they had no outer clothing to keep them warm.

The result of this severity was to polarize people further. Nowadays, with empty churches attended by dwindling congregations, it's hard to capture the mood of the Covenanters who remained fiercely loyal to the strict tenets of the Solemn League and Covenant, refused ritual liturgy and sang the psalms of David in metrical form instead of hymns.

These psalm-singers from the hills spoke the language of Zion in the idiom of Scotland and those who followed them heard the scriptures interpreted by men whose speech pulsed with poetry. Impassioned challenges, wind-tossed above coarse moorland grass, outdid the song of the laverock (lark): 'Away with scrimpet (mean, stingy) sense which constructs aye God's heart to be as his face! Faith is a noble thing; it soars high; it can read love in God's heart when his face frowns!' preached James Renwick, the last Covenanter to die publicly for his beliefs in February 1688.

In 17th-century Scotland, the scaffold became a pulpit for men who died for their faith. 'I would not exchange this scaffold with the palace and mitre of the greatest prelate (bishop) in Britain,' declared a covenanting minister, James Guthrie, to the crowd gathered to watch his hanging in the Grassmarket in Edinburgh on 1 June 1661. He continued:

Blessed be God who has shown mercy to me such a wretch, and has revealed his Son to me, and made me a minister of the Everlasting Gospel... Jesus Christ is my Life and my Light, my Righteousness, my Strength, and my Salvation and all my desire. Him, O him, I do with all the strength of my soul commend to you.

The public display of severed hands and heads at major city gates spoke against the government and for the martyrs, the new saints of the Church. These grisly exhibits fuelled a growing protest against the government which now forced men (and women, who otherwise had no voice in public life) to swear that the king was head of the Church.

This clause, 'head of the Church', brought the Covenanters, controversially, to war, although they were poor and ill-equipped. The covenanting armies were routed, their leaders tortured and executed, after disastrous battles at Rullion Green (28 November 1666) and Bothwell Brig (22 June 1679). 'Brother, die well, it is the last act of faith you will ever be able to do.' These words, spoken by one of the Covenanters dying on the battlefield, were the testimony of many.

One result of religious unrest in Scotland was a notable Scottish presence in mainland Europe. Young men from Catholic families were to be found in France, Poland and Russia. Scots seminaries were founded at Douai, Paris, Rome and Madrid. Protestant Scots fought in Swedish armies. Presbyterians crossed secretly to Calvinist Holland and studied for the ministry there. There were 800 Highlanders in the armies of the Swedish Protestant King, Gustavus Adolphus, which was looked upon as being an exemplary Christian army, rather like Cromwell's New Model Army.

Back at home, the more extreme Covenanting ministers were now praying publicly for the restoration of the true Israel, the Jewish people, and for the fall of the Antichrist, the house of Stewart. One of these men was Richard Cameron, a merchant's son, ordained in Rotterdam. At his ordination one of the ministers, Robert MacWard, let his hand linger on the young man's bent head. 'Behold!' he declared. 'This is the head of a faithful minister and servant of Jesus Christ who shall lose the same for his Master's interest; and it shall be set up before sun and moon in the public view of the world.'

Richard Cameron returned to Scotland and called folk to Christ. And as he preached, he wept:

Our Lord is here this day, saying, 'Will ye take me…?' There may be some saying, 'If I get or take him, I shall get a cross also.' Well, that is true; but ye will get a sweet cross. And what say ye? Will ye take him? Tell us what ye say; for… before these hills and mountains around us we have offered him unto you this day.

Cameron proclaimed war on the king. On 22 June 1680, he rode into the small Border town of Sanquhar with his brother Michael and about twenty men, all armed with pistols. Richard Cameron dismounted, sang a psalm, prayed and read out a declaration of war:

Although we be for government and governors, such as the Word of God and our Covenant allows, yet we for ourselves, and all that will adhere to us, as the representatives of the true Presbyterian Kirk and Covenanted nation of Scotland, do by this present disown Charles Stuart, that has been reigning—or rather tyrannizing, as we may say—on the throne of Britain these years bygone… We also, being under the standard of our Lord Jesus Christ, Captain of Salvation, do declare war with such a tyrant and usurper, and all men of his practices.

This extreme stance made many Presbyterians distance themselves from the Cameronians, and sowed dissension within the ranks of the Covenanters themselves.

A disastrous encounter with government troops followed at Airds Moss in Ayrshire, July 1680. 'Come,' Richard Cameron encouraged his brother, 'let us fight it out to the last! For this is the day I have longed for, and the death that I have prayed for, to die fighting against our Lord's enemies;

and this is the day that we will get the crown.' Then he said to his followers, 'For all of you that fall today I see Heaven's gates cast wide open to receive them.'

Richard Cameron died on the field. His head and hands were cut off and carried to Edinburgh where they were shown to his father, Allan Cameron, a prisoner in the city's Tolbooth. 'Do you recognise these hands?' the soldiers asked, and the old man replied, 'These are my son's, my own dear son's. Good is the Lord who can do no harm to me or mine.'

Richard Cameron's head and hands were then nailed to the Netherbow Port, the gateway into the city above the Tolbooth.

Cameron's example of defiance was followed five years later by another young preacher, James Renwick. 'Is it not more sweet to be swimming in the swellings of Jordan for Christ than to swelter in the pleasures of sin?' asked Renwick, rhetorically, and nailed his own declaration to the market cross, at the centre of the small town of Sanqhar.

Despite his political intransigence, love seems to have been the hallmark of James Renwick's life and it won followers to his cause. 'Love is a resolute soldier; love is an undaunted champion; love's eye is so much taken up with contemplating the Beloved that it cannot see dangers in the way, but runneth blindly upon them, and yet not blindly, because it knoweth for whom and for what it so ventureth,' Renwick declared.

When Renwick was finally captured in Edinburgh, the captain of the guard was amazed to discover the identity of the frail, gentle prisoner. 'Is this boy that Mr Renwick whom the nation has been so troubled with?' he exclaimed.

James Renwick's declaration, like Richard Cameron's, was an act of open rebellion against the government, and the Privy Council retaliated by bringing out an Oath of Abjuration: any man who refused to disown Renwick's declaration was to be hanged, while a woman 'who had been active in the said courses in a signal manner' was to be drowned.

The beautiful hillsides of Galloway bear witness to the faith of the Covenanters. One of these Covenanters was a farmer's daughter, Margaret Wilson, who was eighteen when she was sentenced to be drowned in the Solway Firth at Wigtown, along with her older friend, Margaret Lachlan.

In Scotland, nobles sentenced to death were usually guillotined—

although Montrose was hanged like a commoner. The guillotine was called the Maiden—a black joke, for the man who laid his head upon the block kissed the coldest maiden of all. Women were drowned. Helen Stark had been the first woman martyr of the Scottish Reformation, in 1544. Now Margaret Wilson and Margaret Lachlan were to be the last.

Margaret's father, Gilbert Wilson—'a man to ane excesse conform to the guise of the times'—was punctilious in attending the official churches with the Episcopal clergy and their prayer books, together with his wife. Both were farmers from the Galloway parish of Penninghame, 'in good condition as to worldly things, with a great stock on a large ground'. But their three children, Margaret, Thomas and Agnes, 'being required to take the Test and hear the curates, refused both; were searched for, fled and lived in the wild mountains, bogs and caves'.

The Wilson parents were heavily fined, and soldiers were quartered on their farm, while their outlawed children took what shelter and food they could from the hills and remote sea shores.

Leaving Thomas in the hills, the two sisters went secretly into Wigtown, perhaps because the recent death of Charles II (1685) had brought an easing-off of pressure—or perhaps simply to visit friends, not least an elderly widow, Margaret Lachlan, 'whom they greatly loved and who was well qualified to administer comfort and counsel to them in their troubles'.

Betrayed to the town authorities, the girls were taken to the worst jail the town could offer, 'The Thieves' Hole', and from there they were both transferred to prison where they found that the widow Margaret Lachlan had been arrested too and was sharing the same grim conditions.

The women were brought to a crude trial before five men, two of them notoriously cruel—Sir Robert Grierson of Lagg, who went down in history as 'the devil's own man', and Colonel David Graham, whose royalist brother had clashed with the Covenanters in battle and was known by them as 'bloody Claverhouse'. The two young girls and the simple, elderly widow were charged with being 'out' with the Covenanters at the battles of Bothwell Bridge and Airds Moss (which was complete nonsense). They were also required to swear the Abjuration Oath and declare the king to be head of the Church, thus rejecting the doctrine of the Covenanters.

The women categorically refused to swear the oath and were condemned to be 'tied to stakes fixed in the sand within the floodmark in the Water of Bladnoch near Wigtown, where the sea flows at high water, there to be drowned'.

There was an immediate outcry. Petitions were made to the authorities in Edinburgh. Gilbert Wilson, whose resources were all but squandered, managed to raise £100 and buy the life of his younger daughter, thirteen-year-old Agnes. It seems that a reprieve was in fact issued in Edinburgh ten days before the other two women's deaths, but if so, it didn't reach the unpopular Lagg and Graham. Because of the discovery of this reprieve, various writers have expressed doubt that the women were actually executed, but there is no evidence that the reprieve was ever sanctioned. In 1863 a writer, Mark Napier, put forward 'the case for the crown' and claimed that the women martyrs were a myth. He defended his views in 1870 in a book called *History Rescued*. Napier was answered by Archibald Stewart, who wrote, 'Sense, impartiality and critical sagacity are not only entirely lacking—the writer has no perception of such qualities.'[56]

Local history, not least the Kirk Session records of Kirkinner and Penninghame, signed by elders who had witnessed the deaths, comes down heavily on the side of the following story.

Eighteen-year-old Margaret Wilson was led out to be drowned, along with 67-year-old Margaret Lachlan. A crowd went out from the town of Wigtown to watch the execution. 'The sands were covered wi' cluds o' folk, a' gathered into clusters, many offering up prayers for the women while they were being put down.'[57]

Today a wooden platform leads out over reclaimed saltmarsh to a single stone which marks the approximate place where the women were drowned. Cattle graze where the tide used to race. Eel grass grows here, thrift and glasswort. In the past, glasswort was burned and the ashes were mixed with sand to make glass. Perhaps the two Margarets saw a plume of smoke rising from the shore as they were led into the tideline to the waiting stakes.

Curlews cry now, as they did then; and the hills across the bay would have reminded the women of the high places of Israel, the refuge of the

Everlasting God. And so they sang psalms as they waited for the incoming tide, which flooded rapidly up the course cut by the River Bladnoch where the two stakes had been driven.

Calculated cruelty, or perhaps a desire to persuade the younger Margaret to weaken and agree to swear the Oath of Abjuration, made the officials drive the stakes at a distance from one another so that Margaret Lachlan would drown first, and her death be watched by the eighteen-year-old girl.

They asked Margaret Wilson what she thought at the sight of her friend struggling in the racing tide.

'I see Christ wrestling there,' Margaret replied, and challenged her persecutors in her turn: 'Do you think we're the sufferers? No, not us: it is Christ in us who suffers.'

As she sang the 25th Psalm, the tide rushed higher, but before she was quite dead the soldiers cut her loose. She was choking, sodden, quaking, half drowned as they held her out of the water and asked her to pray for the king. 'I wish the salvation of all men and the damnation of none,' she replied as soon as she could speak.

The crowd pressed closer. 'Dear Margaret, say, "God save the King",' some of them urged, and she answered, 'God save him if he will, for it is his salvation that I desire.'

'She hath said it, oh sir, she hath said it,' the crowd appealed to the officer in charge, but he thrust the Oath of Abjuration at Margaret yet again. 'Swear, or return to the water.'

'I will not swear. I am one of Christ's children. Let me go,' said Margaret and the soldiers thrust her back into the water. 'Tak' anither drink, hinny,' one of them said, shoving her under the waves.

So Margaret died. Her body and that of Margaret Lachlan were buried in a criminals' grave to the north of the old church of Wigtown.

The townsfolk did not forget their deaths. The Wigtown Kirk Session records that on 8 July 1704, nineteen years after the event, the Town Baillie publicly confessed 'the grief of his heart that he should have sitten on the seize of these women who were sentenced to die in this place in the year 1685'. He went on to say 'that it had been frequently his petition to God for true repentance and forgiveness of that sin'.

It was reported that for years after the drowning, a poor, broken man could be seen wandering about the streets of Wigtown, carrying a jug of water everywhere he went, for he was smitten with incurable thirst. People shrank back when they saw him, for he was the man who had mocked Margaret, pushing her back under the waves: 'Tak' anither drink...' Now he would drink and drink and never feel refreshed.[58]

Soon after their deaths, a memorial to each woman was carved on rough slabs where their bodies lay. Other more grandiose memorials followed, in Wigtown itself, in Stirling and Aberdeen, but the most moving memorial is the single stone on the saltmarsh and the endless song of the wind over reclaimed land where geese winter and cattle graze.

But the tides of history were turning. The two Margarets were drowned in 1685, and, in the words of an old lady recounting the story, 'No mony years efter that cam the Revolution, and the ministers was allowed to get on wi' the preaching o' the true gospel withoot the king interfering' ('Not many years after that came the Revolution, and the ministers were allowed to get on with the preaching of the true gospel without the king interfering').[59]

The Revolution that this old lady (another Mrs Wilson) mentions in such a positive light refers to the protracted negotiations after 1688 when James VII (James II of England) fled to France and William of Orange, husband of the deposed Stewart king's sister, Mary, took over the British throne. Scotland negotiated the deal through a Convention parliament. Presbyterianism was officially recognized as the national Church of Scotland, and Episcopacy was outlawed. The religious struggle had lasted 120 years, during which two monarchs and many of the nobility had lost their heads, cities had been sacked and merchants ruined, while ordinary people had suffered incalculable privation and loss. Now at last, the Presbyterians would seem to have come out on top and 'the ministers were allowed to get on with the preaching of the true gospel without the king interfering'. None the less, the story of Christianity in Scotland cannot be summed up as easily as Mrs Wilson had put it and as generations of Presbyterian schoolchildren have been taught. The story was more complex, as our next three chapters will show.

CHAPTER 6

Faith & Massacre, Education & Revival in 18th-Century Scotland

'From Scenes Like These Auld Scotia's Grandeur Springs'

'I would be glad if every girl were to read the Gospel...'

Continue in what you have learned. (2 Timothy 3:14)

The great Renaissance humanist Erasmus of Rotterdam had said in 1516, 'I would be glad if every girl were to read the Gospel and the Epistle of Paul.'[60] The 16th century saw literacy become more widespread, and it has to be pointed out that the post-Reformation achievements in this field were built on the advancements from previous years. Three major Scottish universities were founded before the Reformation. Edinburgh University Old College and

Marischal College in Aberdeen were both established post-Reformation, but lack of funding hampered the progress of basic education generally.

Before the Reformation, the language of education had been Latin, and the classics were to hold sway in higher education until the 19th century. After the Reformation, once the royal Court had moved south to Westminster, English became the language of the Kirk. The Covenanters, we have seen, often used Scots words in their preaching, but the Scots tongue was gradually being displaced by the language of the Authorized Version of the Bible (1611). The psalms, too, in their metrical version, were in English, not Scots. These two factors heralded the decline of Scots as a language. As far as the older language of Scotland, Gaelic, was concerned, the Education Act of 1616 had declared it to be 'one of the chief and principal causes of the continuance of barbarity and incivility among the inhabitants of the Isles and the Highlands' and had decreed that it should be abolished:

Forasmuch as the king's Majesty having a special care and regard that the true religion be advanced and established in all the parts of this kingdom, and that all his Majesty's subjects, especially the youth, be exercised and trained up in civility, godliness, knowledge and learning, that the vulgar English tongue be universally planted, and the Irish (i.e Gaelic) language, which is one of the chief and principal causes of the continuance of barbarity and incivility among the inhabitants of the Isles and the Highlands, may be abolished and removed.[61]

'Barbarity and incivility': the two words sum up the way Lowlanders viewed Gaelic-speaking Highlanders and Islanders. Added to that were 'Popery' and a strong suspicion that the 'savage' men and women of the north were far from loyal to the Crown. Even the landscape put people off. 'The huge naked rocks being just above the heath, produce the disagreeable appearance of a scabbed head,' complained a gentleman called Burt.[62]

THE MASSACRE IN GLENCOE

Our pursuers were swifter than eagles in the sky; they chased us over the mountains. (Lamentations 4:19)

Racial and religious prejudice lay behind an act of ethnic cleansing on 13 February 1692 in the awesome setting of Glencoe. The massacre was a direct result of policies set out by King William of Orange and the Lord Advocate of Scotland, James Dalrymple, 1st Viscount of Stair. On 2 December 1691, Stair wrote to the Earl of Breadalbane, King William's representative in the north:

I think the clan Donell (MacDonald) must be rooted out... God knows whether the 12,000 pounds sterling had been better employed to settle the Highlands, or to ravage them; but since we will make them desperate, I think we should root them out before they can get that help they depend upon.

As we shall see in the next chapter, exactly the same casual racism and brutal logic would be employed against Gaelic-speaking peasants by their 19th-century landlords.

'That's the only popish clan in the kingdom,' wrote Stair to the king (erroneously: the MacDonalds of Glencoe were Episcopalian), 'and it will be popular to take severe course with them. Let me hear from you with the first whether you think that this is the proper season to maul them in the long cold nights... Write your thoughts on the whole with the first, for all must be readiness by the first of January.'

Counting on ancient loyalties to the Crown, William of Orange tried to bind the Highland chiefs to him by personal oath, which had to be taken by New Year's Day 1692. MacIain of Glencoe, Chief of Clan MacDonald, put off the moment of signing as long he could, then rode off to the newly established garrison at Fort William. However, although government forces of 1,200 men were housed behind a wooden palisade, the military commander had no authority to receive the chief's reluctant but compliant oath. MacIain therefore had to set out for Inverary, a distance of close on a hundred miles over rugged hills and mountain passes. The old chief's mistake cost his clan dear—and the delay delighted Stair, who wrote to the king: 'Just now my Lord Argile tells me that Glenco hath not taken the oathes, at which I rejoice, it's a great work of charity to be exact in rooting out that damnable sect, the worst in the Highlands.'

The king, accordingly 'convinced of the necessity of severity', signed an agreement that the MacDonald clan should be 'extirpated root and branch'. Captain Robert Campbell of Glenlyon, a major in the Duke of Argyll's regiment, led the king's troops. Glenlyon's orders were clear:

Yow are hereby ordered to fall upon the rebells, the Macdonalds of Glencoe, and to put all to the sword under 70. You are to have special care that the old fox and his sons do not escape your hands. You are to secure all the avenues, that no man escape… This is by the King's speciall commands, for the good and safety of the countrey that these miscreants be cutt off root and branch.[63]

In actual fact, many of the 200 families escaped—but severe February weather was as merciless as enemy swords, and women and children died in the snow while soldiers torched their homes.

Subsequent enquiries inevitably exonerated the Crown, with the result that the whole guilt of the massacre of Glencoe has been laid squarely on Clan Campbell, even though few of the king's troops were actually Campbells. It has gone down in legend as an act of betrayal, for the MacDonalds had fed and sheltered the king's troops who then abused the ancient laws of hospitality and fell upon their unprepared hosts at 5 o'clock in the morning. The king successfully shielded himself from blame, but the massacre hardly helped his cause in the Highlands.

'AS I SPUN AT MY WHEEL I READ MY BIBLE ON MY KNEE': THE SPREAD OF LITERACY

My tongue is like the pen of a ready scribe. (Psalm 45:1)

It was against the background of mistrust and betrayal that the Scottish Society for the Propagation of Christian Knowledge (SSPCK), established at the beginning of the 17th century, set about spreading education in the English language and Christian civilization (in other words, Presbyterianism) throughout the Gaelic-speaking areas of Scotland.

SSPCK received its charter under Queen Anne in 1709, two years after the Union of the Parliaments (1707), and, with its prejudiced view that 'civilization' meant Protestant and Anglo-Saxon culture, founded 109 schools in the Highlands. The teachers moved from parish to parish, living in filthy huts and teaching Gaelic-speaking children in a foreign language. Vast areas seem to have been left without any provision. In 1775 the Reverend Lachland Shaw reported that 'from Speymouth to Strathspey, from Badenoch Lochiel to Lorne' there was only one school.[64]

As well as SSPCK schools, education was funded by local Presbyterian parishes, and conditions were poor in most 17th- and early 18th-century schools in Scotland. In 1677, for example, the school in Burntisland (across the Forth from Edinburgh) had a seat for the master but no stools or benches for the children, who sat on an earthen floor strewn with heather and grass 'like pigs in a litter'.

In some parishes the schoolmaster and his family lived in the schoolroom itself. The box bed was put in the middle of the floor so that its back acted as a partition behind which the teacher's wife coped with babies and domestic chores while lessons continued on the other side. In the parish of Strathblane in 1717, the Kirk Session reported that pupils couldn't attend school because the roof let in the rain. Scholars were ordered to bring straw to thatch the roof, but straw was so scarce that the parents couldn't provide it.

The schoolmaster was often untrained—and the pittance he earned was often unpaid, particularly in years when harvests were poor. There are frequent reports of church collections having been filled up with debased or foreign coinage, and while this may seem like cheating on God, it is actually a reflection of the level of poverty within Scottish parishes. Often the parish poor eked out some sort of subsistence by going around the doors, begging. It was easier for people to afford a bowl of soup, a dish of ale, an egg or a scrap of clothing than to give money to the Kirk Session. Sometimes the parish could only afford to provide a bowl of porridge a day to the schoolmaster and his family. In 1746 a minister reported that he could not find a teacher because the salary offered by the parish was so low. An old man or an invalid, unfit to work on the farms, a student or a failed minister might end up as a school teacher.

The teacher earned extra money from other offices in the parish: he might keep the register of baptisms and marriages, proclaim the banns, and act as precentor—intoning the first line of the psalms for people to follow. (There were no musical instruments in Scottish churches until organs were introduced in the 19th century.) He could also act as clerk to the Kirk Session, beadle and even gravedigger.

School discipline was strict and could be cruel. This was an age in which even children of the nobility might exist on a diet of near starvation, looked after by a succession of vicious tutors who made their charges endure duckings in cold baths, or locked them in dark cupboards while their 'elders and betters' danced and dined above stairs.

Children had to learn the basic doctrines of Calvinism—the Shorter Catechism, which begins 'What is man's chief end?' and includes 'What doth every sin deserve?' Their answers might well be punctuated by beatings from the tawse, a strap of horse-hide, steeped in brine and divided into cruel fingers, hardened in the fire.

The novelist George MacDonald (1824–1905) gives a picture of a Scottish parish school:

Now there was a little pale-faced, delicate-looking boy in the class who blundered a great deal. Every time he did so the cruel serpent of leather went at him, coiling round his legs with a sudden, hissing swash. This made him cry, and his tears blinded him so that he could not even see the words which he had been unable to read before. But he still attempted to go on, and still the instrument of torture went swish-swash round his little thin legs.[65]

Similarly, describing the education received by his father in the latter half of the 18th century in the parish of Applecross, John Kennedy writes: 'He was taught to read and write and count, and was crammed with Latin. This was all the parish teachers in the Highlands in those days usually tried to do, besides practising themselves in the use of the lash, their kilted pupils affording them a tempting facility for the performance.'[66]

Children had to face the terrors of the schoolroom on the Lord's Day too. The schoolmaster was required to gather children together and 'cause them to read with propriety and decorum passages from Scripture and other devout authors and repeat lectures and texts given by the preacher, as far as their memories and maturities will admit'.

The pulpit was the centre of the church, and sermons were lengthy. The sand might run through the hourglass beside the pulpit one, two, or even three times before the preacher was done. Like the schoolhouse, the floor of a 17th-century Scottish Kirk might be of beaten earth, the congregation sitting on stools, as we have seen, or on the ground. In time, more prosperous parishioners built their private pews. Typically, the laird (local landowner) sat in the gallery, raised above the common folk and eye to eye with the minister in his high pulpit. In Drainie Kirk in Lossiemouth, the space beneath the stair which led to the gallery formed a little room where children were imprisoned for using bad language or 'playing on the Sabbath day'. Drainie Kirk Session Records for 14 November 1722 read:

It was informed that the little house under the stair to the loft in the church was now open, by reason of the door thereof being rotten; and that it were proper it should get a lock, seeing that when it was shut it was ane awband on children for scaring them from playing on the sabbath day and from cursing &c.[67]

An awband was a bridle used to restrain unmanageable cattle. The term was also used in farming communities to describe any kind of restraint on wrongdoers.

THE SPREAD OF LITERACY IN 18TH-CENTURY SCOTLAND

Like newborn babies, crave pure spiritual milk. (1 Peter 2:2)

When he was a small boy, Alexander Carlyle (1722–1805), one of the most brilliant minds of the 18th century, found such a large crowd gathered in his father's church in Prestonpans that he couldn't get in. A small huddle of elderly women were gathered outside and young Alexander offered to read to them. They lifted him on to a tombstone where, as he writes, 'I read very audibly to a congregation, which increased to about a score, the whole of the Song of Solomon.' He was six years old!

Perhaps it's not so surprising that a son of the manse who was also a genius might be able to read; but Thomas Boston of Duns (1676—1732) had none of the privileges of Carlyle—as a young boy, Thomas had visited his Covenanting father in prison. But Boston's ministry influenced the whole of Scotland with the oddly named 'Marrow theology'—a warm assurance of salvation which rested entirely upon Christ and not upon the individual believer. His book, *Human Nature in its Fourfold State*, had an influence second only to the Bible for the next 100 years and encouraged a simple, evangelical faith. Self-taught, he wrote a major treatise on Hebrew, 'his darling study', which was translated into Latin and published after his death.[68]

Testimonies from people from all walks of life show that, however inadequate schools may have been, cheap broadsheets, pamphlets, printed sermons and the Bible found a ready readership in 18th-century Scotland.

Here are entries from the parish records of Cambuslang, near Glasgow, at a time of religious revival. 'I could read the Bible by the time I was six years old,' testified 32-year-old Anne Wylie, and 16-year-old Elizabeth Dykes had a similar story: 'I was taught by my father to read the Bible by the time I was six years of age.'

Archibald Bell told the minister, 'I was born in the Highlands; and my parents living far from any place where there was a school, I was not put to it, nor could I read any till I was about fourteen years of age: and then, in time of my apprenticeship, I got lessons and so came at length to read the Bible.'

People snatched time at work to read. Several girls and women reported, 'As I spun at my wheel I read in my Bible upon my knee.' The 18-year-old daughter of a ship's carpenter from Greenock reported that whenever she picked up her Bible, 'I asked a blessing on what I was going to read in the Bible, that the Lord would give me the sanctified use of it'.

People read devotional books and serious theology too. A young woman of twenty reported how, on her way to draw water from the well, 'I could not forbear taking out Vincent's Catechism to read a little, because I could get no other time for reading. Turning to 1st Peter 2, verses 19–20, the words filled me with so much joy, that I could not forbear skipping for joy.'

Even skipping for spiritual joy was questionable—how much more dancing at fairs and weddings! John Parker enjoyed 'going to fairs and markets and weddings where young people drink and make merry with one another'. But he saw 'the evil of carnal delights, of getting songs and ballads by heart and whistling and singing them over... the matter of these songs not being very chaste oft times, and at best but trifling... therefore I broke off these practices... got some Psalms by heart, or some parts of them, and often sung them when I was following my work... I found myself as much in my element in praising God in this manner, as in whistling and singing before.'[69]

In a letter written in August 1787, Scotland's national poet, Robert Burns (1759–96), names fifteen books which formed the background to his education, a not inconsiderable library which included theological and devotional books. He doesn't mention the Bible—he takes it for granted. Family prayers were also a feature of life in 18th-century Scotland. Burns gives a picture of a peasant family (generally thought to be his own) gathered around the Bible in 'The Cottar's Saturday Night':

> *From scenes like these auld Scotia's grandeur springs,*
> *That makes her lov'd at home, rever'd abroad.*
> *Princes and lords are but the breath of kings.*
> *'An honest man's the noblest work of God';*
> *And certes, in fair virtue's heavenly road,*
> *The cottage leaves the palace far behind...*

It has to be said that Burns tended to stumble on 'fair virtue's heavenly road' and was no stranger to the punishment stool, an essential piece of furniture in 18th-century parishes. The Kirk had inherited the idea of confession and penance from pre-Reformation days and made it a public act.

Literacy and love of the Bible:
'He hath casten me the keys of the pantry-door, and bids me take my fill'

Although Burns satirized the narrow doctrines of the Kirk—and their even narrower adherents—he never attacked the Christian faith. 'A Mathematician without Religion is a probable character; an irreligious poet is a monster,' he wrote in 1788, and two years later, 'We can no more live without Religion, than we can live without air.' And in 1792 he wrote to his son's godmother:

I am so convinced that an unshaken faith in the doctrines of Christianity is not only necessary by making us better men, but also by making us happier men, that I shall take every care that your little godson & every little creature that shall call me, Father, shall be firmly persuaded that 'God was in Christ, reconciling the world unto himself, not imputing unto men their trespasses'.

Burns wrote a paraphrase of Psalm 1 as well as other passages of scripture. In 1787 he wrote, 'I have taken tooth and nail to the Bible, and am got through the five books of Moses, and half way in Joshua. It is really a glorious book.'[70]

Burns was not alone in his love of the Bible. 'There was a poor widow in Clydesdale as I came through,' said Covenanter Alexander Peden. 'When she was asked how she did in this ill time, "I do very well," said she. "I get more good in one verse of the Bible now than I did in it all langsyne. He hath casten me the keys of the pantry-door, and bids me take my fill."'

Daniel Defoe, Selkirk-born government agent and author of *Robinson Crusoe*, returned to his native Scotland for the Act of Union of 1707, accompanying the English Commissioners. He noted how Scottish congregations listened to sermons 'as though they wished to eat the words as they left the minister's mouth'. He added 'a hint to English hearers... In a whole church full of people, not one shall be seen without a Bible... if you shut your eyes when the minister names any text of

Scripture, you shall hear a little rustling noise over the whole place, made by turning the leaves of the Bible.'[71]

'A RUNNING STREAM THEY DARE NA CROSS': WITCH HUNTS IN POST-REFORMATION SCOTLAND

Let no one be found among you who sacrifices his son and daughter in the fire, who practises divination or sorcery, interprets omens, engages in witchcraft, or casts spells, or who is a medium or spiritist or who consults the dead. (Deuteronomy 18:10, 11)

The dark side of the post-Reformation years in mainland Scotland was witch hunting—which was rampant throughout Europe. At the foot of Edinburgh's much-visited Royal Mile, directly opposite Canongate Kirk, which the queen attends, is an old house with white seashells embedded in the stone walls. It was widely believed that witches couldn't cross running water—but there was no water close by and so the householder took the shells for protection. In one of Burns' best-known poems, 'Tam o' Shanter', Tam's 'gray mare, Meg' is advised to do her 'speedy utmost' and get to the bridge ahead of the pursuing 'hellish legion':

> *There, at them, thou thy tail may toss,*
> *A running stream they dare na cross.*

Burns was able to treat the subject of witchcraft with humour, but earlier in the century it was taken very seriously indeed. A kind of mania spread through the country, starting in 1590 when King James encountered a storm at sea as he set out for Denmark to meet his intended bride. The devil wearing a black gown and black hat, 'with claws on his hands and feet shaped like a griffin' was supposed to have helped women said to be witches to raise the storm. The king survived. The supposed witches were killed.

The belief in witchcraft was based on fear and ignorance—although the people who tried the witches were men of substance, land-owning lairds.

Bad harvests in a subsistence economy, disease which failed to respond to well-tried cures, an ailing child or a sudden storm led to poor creatures, mainly elderly women, being tortured and killed. In fact, at least one historian asserts that the number of 'witches' murdered at the end of the 17th century was more than the number of martyrs during the Wars of the Covenant. In one year alone, 1661–1662, as many as 300 had been cruelly executed.[72]

In Edinburgh, witches (or wizards) were thrown into the Nor' Loch, an open sewer, where Princes Street Gardens now lie. Thumbs and feet were tied together. If the victim drowned, she was obviously guilty. If she didn't—and many women floated, buoyed up by their petticoats—she was equally obviously in league with the devil. She was fished out of the water, dragged up to the Castle Esplanade and burnt. A plaque marks the place.

A few notable men were accused of wizardry. One of these was John Napier of Merchiston in Edinburgh. In order to calculate the end times, which many people felt to be imminent, Napier, who died in 1617, invented logarithms. Some of his other inventions were plans for weapons of war not built until the 20th century, including tanks and submarines.

The anti-witchcraft laws were finally repealed in 1736. Indeed, as the century wore on it is said that the broad Scots tongue was becoming narrower ('The conversation of the Scots grows every day less offensive to the English ear,' commented Dr Johnson)—and the narrow religion was becoming broader. The Union of the Parliaments in 1707 was supposed to open English trade outlets to the Scots, but Scotland was never happy with the loss of independence. 'Now there's ane end of ane auld song,' said Chancellor Seafield as the bells of Edinburgh played 'Why should I be sad on my Wedding Day?' Many pulpits up and down the land condemned the merger with a country whose church was ruled by bishops. Burns wasn't happy with the Union either. 'Such a parcel of rogues in a nation!' he lamented.

Many contemporaries noted the social changes that the Union of the Parliaments had brought. Clubs of all sorts mushroomed in the cities. 'Everything was matter of conversation: Religion, Morals, Love, Friendship, good Manners, Dress… The subjects were all new and entertaining,' wrote Elizabeth Mure of Caldwell (1714–95) in her diary.[73]

'Lord pity us, wickedness is come to a terrible height,' lamented Robert Wodrow, minister of Eastwood, and son of the Professor of Divinity in Glasgow when the first theatre was opened, tucked discreetly away in one of the Old Town closes.[74]

Tea drinking was introduced in 1720. It was considered a 'vile drug'— the gentry preferred pailfuls of claret. But by 1750, tea laced with brandy had replaced ale for breakfast. One man lamented, 'I used to be asked if I had my morning draught. I am now asked if I have had my tea.' Whisky too had spread from the north. Some ministers gave a gloomy prognosis: 'The introduction of these baneful articles to the poor of tea and whisky will soon produce the corruption of morals and debility of constitution which are so severely felt in every parish and will soon materially impair the real strength of the population of Scotland.'[75]

As for the university, at the beginning of the century Edinburgh had eight professors and 300 students. Books were chained and padlocked to library shelves and knowledge seemed to have stagnated. But Old Town Edinburgh in the 18th century was innovative and lively—a 'hotbed of genius,' wrote Tobias Smollett. By the end of the century there were 21 professors and 1200 students—and many of these men were studying for the ministry. Out and about in 18th-century Edinburgh, you might meet the great figures of the Scottish Enlightenment: the economist, Adam Smith (1723–90), author of *The Wealth of Nations*; with David Hume (1711–76), the friend of Rousseau and free-thinking philosopher with an international reputation, whose books were banned by the Vatican. You might meet Burns himself, and, until his tragic illness, young Robert Fergusson, arguably a greater poet than the Ayrshire bard. Twenty-four-year-old Fergusson's wretched death in Edinburgh's Bedlam led his friend, Dr Andrew Duncan, to petition the City Fathers to found an asylum where those similarly afflicted with mental illness might meet more humane treatment.

The 18th century saw the defeat of the Jacobite Uprisings, which were attempts in 1715 and 1745 to reclaim the British crown for the Stewart kings who were living in exile in Paris. The last battle ever to be fought on Scottish soil took place at Culloden, near Inverness, on 16 April 1746. Scotland was now part of 'North Britain'. Indeed the street names of the New Town of Edinburgh, architect-designed by James Craig in 1767, are politically correct for the age: Hanover Street, Charlotte Square, George Street and Queen Street all showed Westminster that Edinburgh, a capital without a parliament, was loyal to the Crown, while Thistle Street (for Scotland) is the exact counterpart of Rose Street (for England).

HURRICANES AND BAD HARVEST PRECEDE RELIGIOUS REVIVAL, 1739–42

Fire, and hail; snow, and vapour; stormy wind fulfilling his word. (Psalm 148:8, AV)

As well as political and religious upheaval, the 17th century had seen hunger of Two-Thirds-World proportions. The economy was subsistence level at best and a few bad harvests were sufficient to cause starvation on a large scale. These conditions precipitated emigration on the one hand and the Act of Union on the other. By the 18th century, life was only fractionally less precarious. The year 1739 began with an eclipse of the sun on 13 January, followed by violent storms and extensive damage. In Glasgow the 'turrets of the speir (spire) and battlements surrounding the same' of the High Kirk of St Mungo were blown down. Thatch was torn from roofs; rafters and gables blew away.

William M'Culloch, the minister at Cambuslang (to the south-east of Glasgow), preached on the text from Psalm 148:8: 'Fire, and hail; snow, and vapour; stormy wind fulfilling his word' (AV). 'Will neither the voice of God in the Tempests in the air, nor in the threatnings of devouring fire awaken you?' he asked his congregation—and for some, this was a powerful catalyst towards personal renewal.

That same year the price of grain soared after a summer of scorching heat in some parts of the north and continuous heavy rains elsewhere. There was rioting in Leith, Musselburgh, Prestonpans and in Edinburgh itself in 1740, during which government troops fired on distressed and angry crowds. That winter, frosts were so severe that peats could not be cut; inland waterways were so frozen that wood and coals could not be transported. A contemporary, Janet Hamilton, records in her diary that by spring 'bands of haggard and emaciated women and pale, skeleton-like children (were) creeping slowly among the trees, stripping the branches of the beech of their tender leaves, returning to pick them day by day.' Starving children searched among the miller's husks and gnawed the stems of vegetables from the dunghill.

To the ministers' concern, people seemed indifferent about their spiritual condition. 'I could not see any one turning to the Lord who smote them, or crying to him because of their sins, while they howled upon their beds for bread,' said James Robe, the minister of Kilsyth, near Glasgow, whose parish became a centre for revival.

William M'Culloch of Cambuslang was not known to be a gifted preacher. His son wrote of him that 'though eminent for learning and piety, he was not eloquent... his manner was slow and cautious, very different from that of popular orators.' Indeed, M'Culloch was nicknamed the 'yill' or 'ale' minister, because when he got up to preach, many of the congregation left for the ale-house! But now a new note came into his preaching. Praying societies increased within his parish and a further catalyst towards renewal came in summer 1741 when George Whitfield, an Anglican evangelist, came to Scotland. 'Congregations consist of several thousands,' Whitfield wrote in a letter to a friend. 'Never did I see so many Bibles, nor people look into them, when I am expounding, with such attention.'

Whitfield himself had been influenced by a book written by a young Scots Professor of Divinity, Henry Scougal (1650–78). Esteemed across the bitter denominational divide, Scougal's book, *The Life of God in the Soul of Man*, became a Christian classic. John Wesley gave a copy to George Whitfield who confessed, 'A ray of Divine Light was instantaneously darted in upon my soul, and from that moment, but not till then, did I know that I must be a new creature.'[76]

WHITFIELD'S MESSAGE

Do not fear... your Maker is your husband, the Lord of hosts is his name. (Isaiah 54:4–5, NRSV)

The result of Whitfield's preaching was 'a great visible change' in many congregations as people returned to their home churches to talk about messages which 'came with a dint' into their hearts. One young man reported, 'I felt my heart turn hot and melt and overboil in tears.' Such a spiritual hunger and expectancy was aroused that in Cambuslang on 14 February the kirk was full, 'with many standing for want of seats'. Tears and joy were reported, clapping of hands, beating of breasts, shaking, even falling in a faint—manifestations not normally associated with the Presbyterian way. Crowds of people flocked to Cambuslang, walking great distances; and ministers too came to see what was happening. 'Having resided several days in Mr M'Culloch's house,' wrote one, 'I had occasion to converse with many who had been awakened… some who had been very wicked and scandalous, but now wonderfully changed… Very rude and boisterous before, they now had the mildness and meekness of the Lamb about them.'

Differences between Presbyterians and the dreaded Anglicans were forgotten and there were urgent pleas to Whitfield to return to Scotland. 'I have the greatest regard to that dear Servant of Christ Jesus, Mr Whitfield,' William M'Culloch wrote in a letter. And about his own parish he reported:

I daily see new instances of conviction and conversion… about a hundred and thirty souls here have been wounded with a deep sense of their perishing condition… of which about eighty have been comforted… One was a great debauchee, another a moral young woman; another a boy about eight years of age. The first week this work of God was chiefly among the people of this parish, but these ten days past, it has been particularly among strangers that resort here.

Soon the church became too small to hold the crowds and Communion was celebrated outside in the hills, reminding people of the old days of the Covenanters. Whitfield reported, 'People sat unwearied till two in the morning to hear sermons, disregarding the weather.' Whitfield's sermon on Isaiah 54:5, 'Thy Maker is thy Husband; the Lord of Hosts is his name', made a particular impression on his converts.

'He said he was sent to take a wife for his Master's Son, asking if there was any there that wanted to take Christ for their Husband… and I found my heart made sweetly to agree,' said a young man of 21, while another 'almost cried out for joy at the sweet offers of Christ as husband to my soul, and I was ready to strike hands on the bargain'.

'You might have seen thousands bathed in tears,' wrote Whitfield afterwards, 'some at the same time wringing their hands, others almost swooning and others crying out.'

Revival swept through many parishes in Scotland—and, inevitably, brought about detractors and dissenters. Some people feared the charismatic manifestations and split away. The breakaway Seceders held that these were 'delusions of Satan'. Rational mainstream Presbyterians looked for natural causes. 'We are disposed to imitate the actions of others,' stated the minister who succeeded M'Culloch in Cambuslang. Pamphlets were published for and against the revival. The most rabid of these came from the Cameronians (followers of the militant Covenanters), 'the suffering Remnant of the Anti-Popish, Anti-Lutheran, Anti-Prelatic [bishops], Anti-Whitfieldian, anti-Erastian [church subservient to the state], Anti-Sectarian, true Presbyterian Church of Christ in Scotland'. Whitfield was denounced as 'a limb of anti-Christ... an abjured prelatic hireling... a base English imposter... a wild beast from the antichristian field of England to waste and devour the poor erring people of Scotland'; while his followers were 'drinking the poisonous puddles of prelacy and sectarianism'.

It would seem that it was still possible to roast men and women in the name of religion—with words if not with faggots. However, less than a hundred years after the Killing Time, Whitfield had proved that it was possible to be a brother in the faith and yet belong to a different Christian denomination. On the ecclesiastical front the revival seems to have consolidated the mainstream Church, retaining evangelicals who might have drifted away.

'SAVING CHANGE': THE FRUITS OF REVIVAL

Let the word of Christ dwell in you richly. (Colossians 3:16)

Once the froth and first fire died down, it became possible to assess the results of the revival—and in both Kilsyth and Cambuslang it was noted that nine years afterwards people 'gave evidence, by the piety and consistency of their conduct, of the reality of the saving change that had been wrought in their lives'. There was evidence too of a new appreciation of natural beauty. Creation appeared 'in another manner than before'. Intellectual progress was made, new talents were discovered. Many people confessed that they had learnt to read as a result of the revival. Although Sir John Clerk of Penicuik estimated that the loss of one day's work cost the nation 'eight millions of sixpences', for people 'go a-gadding after conventicles' instead of attending to their gainful employment, many traders in fact put right dishonest dealings. Congregations became more openly loving, marriages were mended and many sad people found a continuing source of strength and comfort. As one young widow put it, it had become her 'constant business to travel between the Redeemer's fullness and my own emptiness'. People were no longer afraid to die. As a 42-year-old woman put it: 'I now consider Death as a messenger to come and call me home to my Lord and Husband, to be where he is.'

Beyond the personal sphere, the sense of belonging to God in a covenant as intimate as marriage gave people a vision for the world beyond their parish. People began to pray not only for revival to spread through the whole land, but for the world at large which was opening up with the spread of colonization. The new evangelistic zeal awakened in the revival led to increased support for foreign mission. Claudius Buchanan, one of the first missionaries to India, was born in Cambuslang in 1766 and baptized by the Reverend M'Culloch. Buchanan was helped to find faith by John Newton (the author of the hymn 'Amazing Grace'). He was ordained in the Anglican Church and went to India as chaplain to the East India Company in Calcutta. He provided money to endow bursaries in British universities to stimulate interest in India.

The interlace of faith can be as intricate as the designs of ancient Irish and Pictish art—and it is to the Highlands and Islands of Scotland that the next chapter will turn.

CHAPTER 7

THE HIGHLAND
CLEARANCES

'Sweepings to Be Gathered Out of the Way'

GIVING IT MEANING:
CARSEWELL'S PLEA FOR A GAELIC BIBLE

They read from the Book of the Law of God, making it clear and giving the meaning so that the people could understand what was being read. (Nehemiah 8:8)

The road from Lochgilphead to Oban winds up a steep hill to Kilmartin with its ancient burial mounds, standing stones, and the historic stone crosses inside the church. Five miles further on, a bridge over the racing brown waters of the River Add leads to an imposing stone ruin, Carnasserie Castle. Roofless, its great hall conjures up images of banquets and music-making. A fine stone fireplace, spiral stairs, a wall privy and an oven set deep within the kitchen fireplace for the baking of bread add to the impression of a way of living that was expansive and humane—and bring the 16th century out of the pages of a history book into a living reality. Perhaps something of the character of the castle's owner moulded the shape of the elegant 16th-century house, one of the first non-fortified houses to be built in Scotland. The owner was John Carsewell, who argued strongly that the Bible should be translated into Gaelic.

Educated at St Andrews University and also a graduate of a prestigious bardic school, Carsewell published *Forim na n-Urrnuidheadh* (*The Form of the Prayers*), the Gaelic translation of the Presbyterian Book of Common Order. The date was 1567 and *Forim na n-Urrnuidheadh* was, importantly, the first ever Gaelic book to come off the printing presses.

Carnasserie Castle stands in Campbell country. Forty miles away is Inverary, the seat of the chiefs of Clan Campbell, who supported the Reformation, two of the Earls of Argyll laying down their lives in the cause. It followed, then, that the vast lands of Clan Campbell—Gaelic-speaking and stretching to the Inner Hebrides, to Mull and Iona, the ancient heartland of Columba—would also espouse the new Presbyterian faith. The support of a powerful patron, in the form of the Earl of Argyll, gave Carsewell's book a tremendous boost.

But Carsewell's work also had major implications for Gaelic literature in setting the standard of Common Classical Gaelic in print as a literary language. John Carsewell wrote for Gaelic-speaking ministers of the Reformed Church but his vision was also for 'the Gaels of Scotland and Ireland' to link together in a new, reformed faith and to possess their own Bible. As he said:

But, furthermore, we, the Gaels of Scotland and Ireland, have ever endured a great disadvantage and deficiency beyond the rest of the world in that we have never before had our Gaelic language in print, as all other peoples in the world have had their tongues and languages in print; and we suffer from a lack greater than all other lacks, in that we do not have the Holy Bible in Gaelic in print, as it is printed in Latin and English, and in every other tongue besides.[77]

In fact, Gaelic-speaking Scotland had to wait until 1801 for a complete Bible. This is a shameful fact, given that one of the basic aims of the Reformers was the Bible in the vernacular. That Lowland Scotland could make an exception for Gaelic shows how strong prejudice was; but in obstructing such a translation, the Kirk actually hindered the progress of the Reformation. Knox and the Scottish Reformers, moreover, used English translations of the Bible and made no attempt to provide a Scots version either, to the detriment of that tongue also.

As we have seen, the Reformation parliament of 1560 made Catholicism illegal (see Chapter 5). Priests found saying Mass were locked in the pillory wearing their vestments; and 1572 and 1574 saw the execution of two priests. The result for the Highlands was that much of the Gaidhealtachd (the Gaelic-speaking area of Scotland) simply lost contact with organized religion and, lacking a priest, the people found themselves without any effective Christian ministry. There was, moreover, a dire shortage of Gaelic-speaking Reformed ministers. Highland chiefs in any case resisted the 'learned and godlie men of goode lyff and confersation' chosen by Edinburgh. The records of the diocese of Argyll and the Isles give an example of the way ministers from the south were intimidated by powerful clan chiefs. On 12 February 1624, the minister's sermon was interrupted with a young man 'armed with a sword, a targe, and a hagbiutt' (a sword, a shield and a halberd) who, 'verie rudlee and with ane awful and fierce countenance' handed the minister a letter from the chieftain of Clanranald, ordering the minister to 'reteir him selff from these boundes and have him hame, utherwayis it sould cost him his lyffe' (in other words: 'Get out or else!').

This piece of prose gives us an authentic picture of the use of Scots at the period, as well as providing an insight into the difficulties English-speaking ministers faced in the Highlands. The Gaelic-speaking west looked, as ever, to Ireland and, even though it was illegal, Roman Catholic aid for the Western Highlands and Hebrides came from across the Irish Sea.

AN OVERLAPPING OF MANY SHARED IDENTITIES

How good and pleasant it is when brothers live together in unity! It is like precious oil poured on the head, running down on the beard. (Psalm 133:1–2)

'We, the Gaels of Scotland and Ireland...' Carsewell had said, stating historic cultural connections which the Reformation, firstly, and then Union with England, would suppress until the present day. On the last St Andrew's Day of the 20th century, a significant newspaper supplement, *Scotland and Ireland*, was published jointly by *The Irish Times* and *The Scotsman*. In an article titled 'An overlapping of many shared identities', Foreign Editor Paul Gillespie explained that up till now 'the tangled history of these two islands' has been concentrated on Anglo-Irish relations. However, with devolved government in Scotland and with religious bigotry giving place to ecumenism, new opportunities for renewing historic links have become possible, not least because both Ireland and Scotland seek a constructive role within Europe.

'BREAKING THE SILENCE OF THE SEAS': MISSIONARY APPROACHES TO GAELIC AND THE GAELS

The islanders showed us unusual kindness. (Acts 28:2)

In the 16th and 17th centuries, the ancient links between Ireland and Scotland were only just coming unstuck, and in July 1624 three Franciscan priests crossed from Antrim to Kintyre. All Gaelic-speaking, the missionaries found an immediate entry into the Hebrides and their journeying took them north to the Uists and eastwards right into Sutherland.

Franciscans were wed to Lady Poverty, but they represented a Church which was becoming increasingly centralized and rigid in its observance of ritual. For example, the Host should be made of fine wheat flour—but the staple diet of the Hebrides was oatmeal. 'The people generally use milk-foods and in summer they have hardly any bread,' wrote Father Cornelius Ward, one of the Franciscan missionaries. The Hebrides and the west coast of Scotland are battered by Atlantic gales. The soil is boggy and often little more than a centimetre thick—thereafter the spade strikes solid rock—so it is little wonder that the missionaries also wrote to Rome requesting that on fast days when dairy products were not supposed to be eaten, people might be allowed to eat cheese, 'because seldom do they have anything else to eat, and it frequently happens that there is none of their own bread or oats or barley available'. They also asked for permission to celebrate Mass without a candle or server.

Converts were even refused communion because there was no bread. The missionaries were forced to travel singly because food shortages in the Highlands and the Isles were so great that they could no longer impose themselves in pairs on their impoverished hosts. One priest noted, wryly, 'The inhabitants have greater taste for military exploits than for food and are content with fare which would be scarcely sufficient for other people when fasting.'

The weather could also impede mission. In 1686 another priest, James Devoyer, reported:

Mr Lea and I went to the island called Sleat, where all are called Protestants except for about fifty Catholics who are dispersed here and there. We stayed twenty days to instruct and prepare this small number for Easter Communion, and to welcome into the faith those who presented themselves. There were ten who did so, and many more would have done if it had not been for a very heavy fall of snow which continued to lie during all the time we were there, so that we could not go from our base to seek them out in their little villages, nor could they come to us, so bad was the weather.[78]

A further picture of lifestyle in the Hebrides in the 17th century comes from a secular traveller, Martin Martin, who reported that in Skye: 'the natives preserve and dry their herring without salt for the space of eight months, provided they be taken after the 10th of September. They take out their guts and hang them by pairs upon a rope made of heath... They eat well and without putrefaction.'

But life was literally at subsistence level and Martin Martin also noted that the cows became 'mere skeletons' after the long winter and were too weak to rise from the ground. The cattle fed on seaweed and could 'distinguish exactly the ebb and flow of the tides'. He found their meat sweet and tender and said that when they were being milked, the girls doing the milking 'sang in the sweetest voices'.

A hundred years later, when travel to Scotland was respectable, if a touch exotic, William Wordsworth (1770–1830) was moved by the singing of 'yon solitary Highland lass'. But in the 17th and 18th centuries, the 'farthest Hebrides'—and the Gaelic-speaking Highlands generally—were viewed by Edinburgh and Westminster as an uncivilized abode of 'savages', a hotbed of 'Popery' and Jacobite rebels; and this influenced the negative way the Kirk approached the evangelization of the north.

'THE LAD BORN TO BE KING': THE JACOBITE UPRISING, 1745

Despised by Lowlanders, Gaelic-speaking people of the Highlands and Hebrides had good cause to look to the court of the Jacobites in France rather than to Westminster. Charles Edward Stuart (Bonnie Prince Charlie), the son of the uncrowned James VIII, arrived at Eriskay in the Outer Isles and raised his standard at Glenfinnan, fifteen miles west of the government stronghold, Fort William. Although Charles hoped to draw on Catholic sympathies, and in fact wore the cassock of a French parish priest rather than Highland dress when he first arrived in Scotland, it is the opinion of Professor Michael Lynch that because of inroads made by the SSPCK and internal splits within the Catholic mission, 'Roman Catholics were no more likely to rise in the '45 than Episcopalians, who predominated in a ratio of about seven to three'.[79]

Charles Edward and his army marched south to Edinburgh, where he failed to take the castle, but stayed in Holyrood Palace for a month, trying to increase his army. He marched south to Derby, a mere 127 miles from a panic-stricken Westminster. Ill-advised, he turned back and was routed at Culloden, five miles east of Inverness, on 16 April 1746.

The Hanoverian army under the command of William Augustus, Duke of Cumberland, younger son of George II, slaughtered the wounded on the field with calculated cruelty. 'Butcher' Cumberland, as he became known, left a trail of carnage across the west as his soldiers hunted the prince, the latter being over-fond of his dram even then. (He was to become an alcoholic.) In Ardnamurchan, the most westerly point of the

Scottish mainland, for example, the family of Alasdair MacMhaighster Alasdair, one of the greatest of all Gaelic poets and former SSPCK school-teacher, who had thrown in his lot with the prince, were evicted from their home, and their house was burnt down. (There were many more such burnings to come in the Highland Clearances a hundred years later.)

The followers of the prince, once captured, were transported in dire conditions to the tobacco plantations in America; others were hanged or beheaded. Tartan was forbidden by an Act of Parliament, the Highland Disclothing Act.

In the aftermath of the 1745 Jacobite Uprising, many of the old Highland chiefs were dispossessed, or forced to sell their ancient lands to men from the south. The great divorce between the Gaelic-speaking clansmen and new, English-speaking landlords was already beginning.

However, although a lock of the prince's hair might be a family heirloom, treasured and handed down through the generations, the Jacobite threat to Westminster had receded. The prince himself, back in exile in France, became seriously alcoholic. His brother Henry became a Cardinal. The ancient Stewart line had died and the whole episode could begin to be regarded with the aura of romance. An Episcopalian bishop, Robert Forbes, imprisoned in 1746 for his involvement in the Jacobite cause, wrote a three-volume account of the Highland genocide, *The Lyon in Mourning*. It was published in a shortened version in 1835. The full version appeared only at the end of the 19th century, and by then the whole Uprising, including the prince's escape with the help of Flora MacDonald, was viewed in glowing technicolour.

Episcopalians, outlawed after 1688, and viewed with suspicion during the Jacobite Uprising, were becoming respectable, in Edinburgh at least, partly because of the popularity of Sir Walter Scott, himself an Episco-palian. Up north, however, because of their connection with the landlords on the one hand and their prayer books and vestments on the other, they were still viewed with great suspicion by Presbyterian ministers and their flock. An account of 18th-century religious revival in Ross-shire by Dr John Kennedy, published in 1861 and still read today, mocked an Episcopal church as 'the synagogue of Satan':

In stalked a man who seemed to have come straight from his bed, for he had on his nightgown. The poor man must have been crazy, for who in his senses would come in such a plight before a congregation? Turning towards the people he began to read some gibberish out of a book.[80]

'GOD SAVE THE KING'

I urge, then, first of all, that requests, prayers, intercession and thanksgiving be made for everyone—for kings and all those in authority. (1 Timothy 2:1–2)

By 1764, 6000 Highland Catholics had joined the British Army and this in turn led to the passing of the Catholic Relief Acts which gave Catholics freedom of worship and the right to hold property. By 1795, Catholics were praying for George III at Sunday Masses, and in 1822 George IV visited Scotland. This was the first visit by a reigning royal for over 170 years. The whole thing was carefully stage-managed by the popular novelist Sir Walter Scott. It was a skilful piece of public relations which has left its mark on Scotland to this day, for the Scottish novelist persuaded the monarch (nephew of 'Butcher' Cumberland) to squeeze his great girth into tartan. However, George IV did not wish to display his knees, and came to the capital wearing pink silk tights under his kilt. His statue on the crossing of Hanover Street and George Street commemorates the visit—and shows the monarch with wrinkles around his knees.

Tartan, proscribed along with bagpipes after the '45, became the fashion, and Scotland became the romantic place to visit, an aura which still surrounds it. Queen Victoria set the seal on it all by favouring Balmoral and touring around Scotland. Yet at exactly this time, the Gaelic-speaking people of the Highlands and Islands of Scotland were being driven from their land, displaced in favour of sheep. In Chapter 1, I asked, 'Where are the Gaelic-speaking people of Scotland?' The question is a bitter one—and the answer is harsher still. The stark facts are glossed over in a welter of 'westering home' with a 'swing o' the kilt' among the 'bonnie blooming heather'. Versions of blessings and work-songs intoned by women are published in English in attractive little books. But where are the women? Where are their daughters and granddaughters? Where are the men? Where is the sound of their language?

THE 'GRAND IMPROVEMENT... MUTTON IN LIEU OF MEN': THE HIGHLAND CLEARANCES

For he never thought of doing a kindness, but hounded to death the poor and the needy and the brokenhearted. (Psalm 109:16)

In the wake of the Jacobite Uprising, many impoverished clan chieftains either sold their land to newcomers or became commercial landlords themselves, living in London and the south, marrying Lowland and English wives. The answer for their economic betterment lay not in the soil—but in sheep. Armies march on their stomachs. The Napoleonic Wars (in which Highlanders served with distinction) produced a demand for wool and mutton and made Highland landlords anxious to apply new sheep-farming methods to their estates. They looked on themselves as improvers. Their impoverished tenants, in heather-thatched hovels that they shared with their animals, were an inconvenience and would have to be moved.

A letter from the Earl of Seaforth summed up the landlords' view. 'If it becomes necessary for me, as I fear it will, to carry through the measure of dispossessing a population overgrown and daily becoming more burdensome, to pave the way for the grand improvement of the introduction of mutton in lieu of men...'.[81]

The people were moved to smallholdings on the least productive parts of the estate—so that families would be forced to work for the landlord on his estates—or in the kelp industry. Kelp or seaweed was used to manufacture soap and glass. By 1760 this was a boom industry in coastal areas and landlords made vast profits: the labour force consisted of tens of thousands of families who cut, gathered, dried and burnt seaweed from April until August for minimal wages, neglecting their own poor strips of land as a result. The kelp-gatherers often worked many miles from home, up to their waists in the cold sea, returning to a supper of oatmeal and water and to sleep on the earthen floor of a poor hut.

The workers' misery was all the worse because their employers were their landlords, who kept pushing up rents. Traditionally, the Highland chiefs had been protectors of their people. But the old ways had changed. 'It is impossible I can forego the present rent without extreme inconvenience to my affairs,' wrote Lord Macdonald in 1817. His attitude was typical of the landowners of the day.

Even when the Countess of Sutherland—her conscience pricked by articles in the English press about starvation on her estates—returned to her Gothic pile, Dunrobin Castle, to find out how her tenants lived, she was assured by the Moderator of the Presbytery of Tongue, 'When other districts were left to the precarious supplies of a distant benevolence, your Grace took on yourself the charge of supporting your people. By a constant supply of meal you not only saved them from famine but enabled them to live in comfort.'

Nothing could be further from the truth. Although she was the hereditary chief, the Duchess of Sutherland spoke no Gaelic and never found out that for the last forty years her people had endured cruelty and deprivation which have irredeemably blackened the name of the duke and duchess and of the estate manager Patrick Sellar, who brutally evicted the people from Strathnaver and Kildonan. The Royal Family and other wealthy people now shoot deer where, once, whole communities were forced from their homes with no provision made for their needs.

Other landowners were as ill-informed as the duchess. Lord Seaforth's manager confessed, 'I had no idea of the great hardships and privations that the poor people endure who are forced to new allotments without matters being previously arranged for their moving. The situation of the new cottars in the Aird of Tong at this moment beggars belief.'[82]

The result was mass emigration from the Highlands and Islands. The landlords, however, fearful of losing their workforce, called on the government to act. In 1803, the Passenger Vessels Act put a limit on the number of passengers a ship could carry and pushed up the price of a ticket by 300 per cent, making it impossible for the poor to leave. Emigration stopped and 'these poor people, unable to go to America, are glad to get any sort of plot and hut,' wrote one of the lairds, MacKenzie of Coll in 1813.[83]

'OF GREAT SERVICE TO THE COUNTRY': THE RIDDELL PAPERS AND KIRK SESSION RECORDS OF ARDNAMURCHAN

He who rebels against authority is rebelling against what God has instituted. (Romans 13:2)

Until the mid-19th century, the parish church was almost the only source of poor relief, particularly in rural areas. However, the ministers of the Church of Scotland, the providers of poor relief, were firmly on the side of the landlords, as we saw from the bland untruths told by the Moderator of Tongue. Citing Romans 13:2, many ministers told the people that to resist the evictions, which were carried out in the name of the Law, was to resist the will of God.

Everywhere, from Sutherland to Lewis, people were forced off fertile land to eke a new existence in poor coastal areas. The laird's men made people milk the cows, and then poured the milk over the peat fire—which was never normally allowed to go out. They set fire to the heather thatch so that anyone who dared return would have no roof over the heads. Blue smoke rose into the air—on a clear day, this was a sign for miles around that a township was being 'cleared'. And the people, old and young, starving and destitute, sick or well, were driven away with their cattle to fend for themselves as best they could. At nightfall they would seek some sort of shelter—but the cows could give no more milk. This kind of behaviour caused the landlords, traditionally protectors of their people, to be seen in the light of the wicked man in the psalm quoted earlier: 'For he never thought of doing a kindness, but hounded to death the poor and the needy and the brokenhearted' (Psalm 109:16).

Contemporary records of the Kirk Session of Kilchoan Parish Church in Ardnamurchan reveal the extreme poverty of tenants on that beautiful windswept peninsular, the most westerly point of the Scottish mainland.

St Coan, a monk from Iona, had evangelized here: an ancient standing stone from pre-Christian times is inscribed with a cross as evidence of the change. It stands by the sea in beautiful Camus-nan-Gall (the Bay of Gael), overlooking the Sound of Mull. Roofless stone cottages bear witness to a community swept away by the 'progress' of a more modern age.

At the end of the 18th century, the estates of Ardnamurchan and Sunart had been bought by Sir James Riddell, Bart. The baronage of Scotland describes him as 'well-skilled in the English method of agriculture and improving of ground... which example will be of great service to the country.'[84]

James Riddell had his estate surveyed in 1807. This survey assessed the suitability of land for sheep, not the living conditions of the people. It callously calculates the 'necessary' eviction of the tenants:

It would seem proper to reduce the number of Tenants which would give the arable part of this land a chance of being better managed... Both farms together would make a good Sheep Walk, fit for Cheviot Sheep, but the junction would occasion the removal of a number of poor tenants... Soil is thin, though it is under a pretty good crop this year. It is also oppressed with a number of Tenants.[85]

And so the lands were cleared on Ardnamurchan as elsewhere. Sir James Riddell was praised as a 'humane and kindly proprietor' who held back evictions and was patient with rent arrears. *The Edinburgh Advertiser* of 25 January 1789 reports that the 'Society for the Relief of the Industrious Poor received from Sir James Riddell of Ardnamurchan, Bart, the sum of £25 sterling. The same day, the above benevolent gentleman sent £5 sterling (for) the purchase of coals for use of prisoners in the Tolbooth.' The same paper also carried a report of the death in a duel of Sir James' 24-year-old son George, of the Horse Grenadier Guards, and the *Edinburgh Courant* adds, 'The situation of Sir James Riddell as a parent is truly pitiable. He never had but two sons, and both of them met a death equally calamitous.'

In fact, Riddell's agents carried out the Clearances in such a heartless way that legend has it that one of them was cursed. Perhaps it was this man who, in 1828, locked a half-witted woman into her cottage. The woman held out until her store of food was exhausted and then, starved into submission, she let the laird's man have her home.

DO YOU THINK YOU WILL WIN DELIVERANCE BECAUSE OF YOUR SHEEP AND ALL YOUR FOLDS?

The old woman is commemorated in a poem by a contemporary, a local doctor, John MacLachlan, who has gone down in the annals of the parish as a colourful character, a fine poet and a man of compassion. John MacLachlan was filled with sorrow at the sight of ruined, roofless cottages where, so recently, whole communities had lived. He appeals to the landlord to consider his actions in the light of God's justice: 'Just consider, when you pass from us, how the King of All will reward you… Do you think you will win deliverance because of your sheep and all your folds?'[86]

The parish register of Kilchoan is a valuable social document. Dating back to 1779 and written in English in neat handwriting, it details the amount, not of money, but of oatmeal, to be divided amongst the poor. The record shows the desperate need of the poor, who were classified as 'objects of charity'—or simply 'objects'. It also lists the causes of poverty: cripple; blind; ill; totally disabled; deaf; very elderly; deaf and dumb; deranged; paralysed. The catalogue also lists a 'changeling', showing how belief in the supernatural was still in vogue, for a changeling was a failing, invalid child, reputedly a replacement for a healthy one snatched away by fairies.

The dead were also cared for by the Kirk: linen for the shroud and plain wooden coffins were provided out of Kirk funds. The Session records show how the Scottish parish provided education and social services—and even acted as a local police force, fining the delinquent. Funding came from donations from the landowner, from marriage fees and fines.

The register for 1837 notes payment for 'board and lying-in charges for Christy MacLean and her Bastard Twins'. In 1839 her 'board' was still being paid for by the Session, but in 1851 Christy MacLean, together with two children, are on another list. They were to be shipped to Australia, victims of the 'final solution' to the extreme poverty of the Highlands. Such emigration was regarded as entirely appropriate by landlords, clergy, government officials—everyone except the people themselves.

THE GREAT HUNGER HITS SCOTLAND

Because of thirst the infant's tongue sticks to the roof of its mouth; the children beg for bread, but no one gives it to them. (Lamentations 4:4)

The profits from kelp were short-lived. When the industry collapsed, Duncan Shaw, who managed Clanranald's Hebridean estates, decided that a shift should be made from kelp to sheep farming, and that 3000 people must be shipped to America. But Scotland was now entirely under sheep and so there was a slump in the price of wool and mutton too. To add to the misery, wet summers produced a blight in the potatoes in the Highlands and Hebrides, as well as in Ireland. The result was famine. People ate grass. 'Bhiodh 'ad a' roinn a' bhloinigein an uair sin' ('They were dividing wild spinach at that time'), it was said.

Newspaper reporters, not hitherto sympathetic to the crofters, were quickly on the scene. *The Inverness Courier* and *The Scotsman* produced regular columns detailing the famine of 1845.

The scene of wretchedness which we witnessed as we entered on the estate of Col. Gordon was deplorable, nay heart-rending… I never witnessed such countenances—starvation on many faces—the children with their melancholy looks, big looking knees, shrivelled legs, hollow eyes, swollen-like bellies. God help them, I never did witness such wretchedness.

So wrote a respected Church of Scotland minister, Revd Norman MacLeod, a forebear of George MacLeod of Iona.

A Board for Relief of the Destitute was set up; but practical necessity—how to feed a population which was now entirely without food—clashed with Victorian social policy. 'Next to allowing people to die of hunger, the greatest evil that could happen would be their being habituated to depend upon public charity. The object to be arrived at, therefore, is to prevent the assistance being productive of idleness and if possible to make it conducive to increased exertion,' said Sir Charles Trevelyan, Assistant Secretary to the Treasury.

So meal was distributed in return for eight hours' work per day, six days a week. Starving families were set to public works—road-making, for example—the women and children carrying the stones which the men laid into paths they had dug with difficulty over areas where the soil is a bare centimetre thick. Women knitted as they carried heavy creels of boulders bound on straps across their foreheads. 'They have to walk, often without shoes and always insufficient clothing... after working eight hours they receive the value of one and a half pence,' wrote Emily MacLeod in a letter, while *The Inverness Advertiser* reported that the 'cruel and demoralizing principle has been to exact a maximum of labour for a minimum of wages'.

The Free Church of Scotland (established after the Great Disruption in 1843, which will be dealt with in the next chapter) set up a fund for the destitute. An eye-witness, Lady MacCaskill, wrote:

At the appointed time and place the poor creatures troop down in hundreds, wretched and thin, starved and wan. Some have clothing, some almost none, and some are a mass of rags. Old and young, feeble and infirm, they take their stations and await their turn. Not a murmur, not a clamour, not a word—but they wept aloud as they told their miseries.[87]

'TO DISPERSE THE PEOPLE AND PUT SHEEP IN THEIR PLACE'

By the rivers of Babylon we sat and wept when we remembered Zion. There on the poplars we hung our harps... How can we sing the songs of the Lord while in a foreign land? (Psalm 137:1–2, 4)

The landlords responded to the famine by shipping away entire populations of 'surplus and useless people… like sweepings to be gathered out of the way,' as Revd D. McCallum of Duirnish put it, in a further wave of clearances which the people could neither influence nor control.

It has been estimated that 50 per cent of the population of the Hebrides and the western coasts of Ardnamurchan and Knoydart was evicted in the ten years between 1846 and 1856: four inhabitants out of every ten were forced on board the waiting ships.[88]

The spiritual aspect of this was a deep sense of betrayal. As we have seen, the clergy mostly supported the landlords and the status quo. However, evangelical mission and religious revival, which we shall discuss more fully in the next chapter, were beginning to give people in the Highlands a voice within their own community. As a result, the newly formed Free Church emerged in the Highlands and Islands as the Kirk of the people, while the national Church of Scotland was discredited for its refusal to stem the evictions.

Writing in 1861, Dr John Kennedy, Free Church minister at Dingwall, whose attack on the Episcopalians was noted earlier (p. 115), contrasts the callous oppression of the 'ungodly oppressors' with people who, far from being 'barbarians', had become 'peaceable and virtuous' as a result of their evangelical faith. He also noted that as the families were being evicted, their menfolk were laying down their lives for the British Crown:

Swayed by the example of the godly… the body of the people in the Highlands became distinguished as the most peaceable and virtuous peasantry in Britain. It was just then that they began to be driven off by ungodly oppressors, to clear their native soil for strangers, red deer, and sheep. With few exceptions, the owners of the soil began to act as if they were also owners of the people, and… families by hundreds were driven across the sea, or were gathered, as the sweepings of the hillsides, into wretched hamlets by the shore… Meanwhile, their rulers, while deaf to the Highlanders' cry of oppression, were wasting their sinews and their blood on battlefields that, but for their prowess and their bravery, would have been the scene of their country's defeat.[89]

People were shipped to Canada (Manitoba was held out as a great attraction), to Australia, to New Zealand. Place names such as Nova Scotia in Canada and Dunedin in New Zealand represent the longing of exiles for home. But it must be remembered, people did not leave willingly, seeking adventure or a better life in a foreign land. They were the victims of a deliberate, oppressive policy based on the survival of the fittest which callously aimed to eliminate the poor. Land had become a resource to be exploited for the profit of the owner. The end result was to make the Highlands unviable economically.

The overriding sense was of sorrow and loss. These words from a Tiree man sum up the way many felt: 'When that morning came when they were to go to a strange land, and every friend in the place had gathered, I cannot express the sorrow that weighed me down.'[90]

The people left in ships which social reformers of the day said were worse than those used by slave traders. Many vessels were hardly seaworthy. Thousands died of disease on the way. The sails dipped beyond the horizon and the ebb tide was filled with the bleating of sheep.

CHAPTER 8

REVIVAL & MISSION
IN THE 19TH CENTURY

'Scotland Shall Be a Garden All in Flower!'

Gather the people, consecrate the assembly; bring together
the elders, gather the children, those nursing at the breast…
And afterward, I will pour out my Spirit on all people.

JOEL 2:16, 28

The typical picture of Scottish 19th-century church life is straitlaced, tight-lipped and dour. However, 'They were grave, but not gloomy,' writes Revd John Kennedy of Highland Christians.[91] Intimate fellowship meetings became the mark of a revived community in the Highlands. These fellowship meetings had begun as early as 1654 in Easter Ross under the ministry of Thomas Hog, who has been described as 'a man of international stature' and 'a great statesman'. Exiled to Holland, like so many Scots Calvinists, he was influential in bringing William of Orange to the British throne.[92]

Hog's idea of small fellowship gatherings spread to other congregations and became a distinctive mark of Highland Presbyterian spirituality.

A great breakthrough for evangelical Christianity in the Highlands came with the long-delayed arrival of the Gaelic Bible at the beginning of the 19th century. Schoolmasters and lay missionaries taught old and young to read the scriptures, newly available in the native tongue. The Gaelic schools also unlocked the scriptures and people were touched so deeply that it seemed that the Day of Pentecost had occurred all over again. One schoolmaster, John MacLeod, sparked off a major revival on the Isle of Lewis in 1823 when he taught old and young alike to read the scriptures in their own language. He explained the Bible to them and the whole community was enthused and inspired. They carried their Bibles with them wherever they went—at home, out in the fields, walking across the hillsides. And contemporary observers noted, 'A very remarkable change has taken place. All known sin is forsaken; and all known duty is observed.'[93]

Revival was infectious. News of an 'awakening' in one fellowship led to others longing for the same deeper experience. The 19th century saw enormous gatherings of the faithful, meeting out-of-doors, whatever the weather. One of the great 19th-century Gaelic preachers was the Revd Dr John MacDonald of Ferintosh. It has been estimated that 9500 people attended his open-air communions and an eye-witness wrote to Sir Walter Scott, 'I can compare the singing to nothing earthly, except it be imagining what would be the effect of a giant Aeolian harp with hundreds of strings.'[94]

An eye-witness at another such gathering in Perthshire in 1816 reported, 'The preaching of Mr Macdonald was accompanied by a power such as they had never witnessed before. The whole congregation seemed affected by a singular movement. I suppose it was something like what the Prophet saw in a vision—a shaking among the dry bones in the valley.'[95]

The year of the Lewis revival (1823) was called *Bliadhna na Aomaidh* ('The Year of the Swooning'). Great emotion was released and people would cry out and even fall into a faint. An entire congregation might 'melt into tears... and such has been the effect on the preacher himself that he has to stop and weep with them'.[96]

'A GENTLE MESSAGE':
THE MINISTRY OF ROBERT MURRAY MCCHEYNE

For to me, to live is Christ and to die is gain. (Philippians 1:21)

Saints canonized by Rome fell out of favour after 1560, but the Reformed faith was not slow in gathering men and women who were held in particular veneration. The martyrs of the Covenant, the great preachers of revival, the missionaries who laid down their lives for the gospel were not formally hallowed, but their fame was handed down by each succeeding generation. The Revd Robert Murray McCheyne, a leading evangelical within the Church of Scotland who died at the age of 29 on 25 March 1843, became a much-admired figure. His brief life was recorded by his friend, Revd Andrew Bonar, in a biography which has become a spiritual classic, reissued many times since its original publication in 1844. Andrew Bonar himself was involved with Robert McCheyne in a 'school of saints' which fostered personal holiness in a spiritual movement of unparalleled intensity.

Robert McCheyne was born in Edinburgh on 21 May 1813. The death of his elder brother David made an enormous impression on 18-year-old Robert. He remembered the anniversary each year: 'On this morning last year came the first overwhelming blow to my worldliness,' he wrote in his diary. Ten years later he wrote, 'This day eleven years ago, I lost my loved and loving brother, and began to seek a Brother who cannot die.'

Robert McCheyne's diary reveals his spiritual life. An entry from his student years in Edinburgh reads: 'February 23—Sabbath—Rose early to seek God, and found him whom my soul loveth. Who would not rise early to seek such company? The rains are over and gone. They that sow in tears shall reap in joy.'

Andrew Bonar writes, 'His whole ministry was little else than a giving out of his inward life... His heart was filled, and his lips then spoke what he felt within his heart. He gave out not merely living water, but living water drawn at the springs that he had himself drank of.'

'Surely it is a gentle message,' Robert wrote of the gospel, 'and should be spoken with angelic tenderness, especially by such a needy sinner.'

Robert was ordained an assistant minister in Larbert, near Stirling. Coal-mines and ironworks polluted the air. He became ill with chest pains and severe respiratory disease, so that he had to give up work for a while, a major frustration for a young man at the outset of his ministry. Robert bore the setback patiently, as a sign of his unworthiness to be a minister and his nothingness before God.

Here are more entries from his diary:

Today sought to prepare my heart for the coming Sabbath… examined my heart with prayer and fasting… Lord, thou knowest all things—thou knowest that I hate all sin, and desire to be made altogether like thee. It is the sweetest word in the Bible—'sin shall not have dominion over you'. O then, that I might lie low in the dust—the lower the better—that Jesus' righteousness and Jesus' strength alone be admired. Felt much deadness and much grief… Towards evening revived. Got a calm spirit through psalmody and prayer…

Evening—Somewhat helped to lay Jesus before little children in his beauty and excellency. Much fatigue, yet some peace. Surely a day in thy courts is better than a thousand.

A year later, Robert McCheyne was called to St Peter's in Dundee, a large parish of 4000 souls, very many of whom never attended any church of any denomination. His congregation consisted of 1100 regulars, one-third of whom came from far afield—and all needed to be visited. His diary lapsed, but his prayer life continued unabated. On Saturday nights he would pray for his parish and for his fellow ministers. On Sunday he would invariably 'rise a great while before day'—not to put last-minute touches to his sermon, but to meditate and pray. Churches where he preached were overcrowded. An old servant of the manse recalled:

He preached in the church on 'Lest I myself should be a castaway,' and the folk were standin' out to the gate, and the windows were pulled down so that those outside might hear… They stayed at the kirk that nicht till eleven. The folk couldna gi'e ower listenin', and Mr McCheyne couldna gi'e ower speakin.' ('They stayed in church that night till eleven. The people couldn't stop listening and Mr McCheyne couldn't stop speaking.') … Oh, to hear Mr McCheyne at prayers in the mornin! It was as if he could never gi'e ower, he had sae muckle (so much) to ask. Ye would hae thocht (have thought) the very walls would speak again. He used to rise at six on the Sabbath mornin', and go to bed at twelve at night, for he said he likit (liked) to have the whole day alone with God.

Not surprisingly, Robert suffered another breakdown in health. While he was convalescing, plans were made that he, Andrew Bonar and two other ministers should make a journey to Palestine. The visit was not, of course, for mere tourism. He wrote to Andrew Bonar, 'Pray for us... that we may be blessed to win some souls, and to stir up Christians to love Zion.'

The trip had the blessing of Robert's doctors, as he explained to his people in Dundee: 'God has plainly shown me that I may perform a deeply important work for his ancient people, and at the same time be in the best way of seeking a return to health.' He also said, 'We should be like God in his peculiar (particular) affections; and the whole Bible shows that God has ever had, and still has, a peculiar love to the Jews.'

The proposed trip excited 'very great' interest in Scotland, as Andrew Bonar explained:

Nor was it merely the somewhat romantic interest attached to the land where the Lord had done most of his mighty work; there were also deeper feelings of a Scriptural persuasion that Israel was still 'beloved for the fathers' sake'... for some time previous Jerusalem had come to mind and many godly pastors were standing as watchmen over its ruined walls (Isaiah 62:6) stirring up the Lord's remembrances.

Herein lay the beginning of a Scottish presence in the Holy Land which continues to the present day. Robert Murray McCheyne's trip would also lead to the establishment of the Jewish Mission in Budapest. The Hungarian connection came about when one of Robert's party, Dr Black, fell off his camel. The accident led to his premature departure. His journey home saw him sailing up the Danube and discovering 'an open door' in Budapest. Steeped in the scriptures, Robert Murray McCheyne and Andrew Bonar found that each new scene, each new encounter with local people, brought some facet of the Bible alive. Their journal has been reissued as *Mission of Discovery* (Christian Focus Publications, 1996). It is an enthralling travel book in its own right.

Robert and his party later returned across Europe, to discover that revival had broken out in Kilsyth and in Dundee with 'much melting of heart and intense desire after the Beloved of the Father'. The church was full to overflowing; people sang as he had never heard them sing before and afterwards he was surrounded by a 'happy multitude', all wanting to shake hands with him and hear him speak.

Revival and foreign mission added to Robert Murray McCheyne's workload. But within the Kirk itself, dissension would lead in 1843 to the Great Disruption and the birth of the Free Church. The issue was over government patronage. Evangelical clergy were anxious that ministers should feel called to a congregation and that the congregation likewise should feel that their minister was one whom the Lord, and not some secular patron, had chosen. Another difficulty was church extension. Evangelicals warmly supported the scheme to build new churches— 'cisterns', as they put it, for the showers that would fall from heaven when the Spirit's anointing came down upon preacher and people alike. During a meeting about church extension, Robert put his thoughts into verse:

> Give me a man of God the truth to preach
> A house of prayer within convenient reach,
> Seat-rents the poorest of the poor can pay,
> A spot so small one pastor can survey,
> Give these—and give the Spirit's genial shower,
> Scotland shall be a garden all in flower!

Pew rents were also a cause of division: the evangelicals favoured rents within the price range of the 'poorest of the poor'; other ministers pointed out that the rents, socially divisive though they might be, were a useful source of money. Church extension too cost money. The established Church looked to the government for grants; the evangelicals were opposed to the involvement of the government in the affairs of the Church. The two factions were irreconcilable. The Great Disruption occurred on 18 May 1843 and the established Kirk was split in two.

THE GREAT DISRUPTION

The Disruption was led by Thomas Chalmers (1780–1847). Chalmers' first charge was the peaceful fishing community of Anstruther in Fife, but from there he moved to Glasgow. In the social upheaval brought about by the Industrial Revolution, Chalmers, drawing upon his experiences in Anstruther, declared that the revival of the nation depended on building up small communities within the parishes.

Chalmers approached the government for assistance in building new churches—but God and Caesar have ever been in conflict. Extra funds were conditional on the government—and not the local congregation—appointing the minister. In 1843, Chalmers, presiding over the General Assembly, in a breathtaking moment led ministers out from the institution they now saw as hopelessly corrupt to form a new Church which took root very strongly in the Highlands and Islands.

The growth of the newly formed Free Church was startling. Of the 1195 ministers in the Church of Scotland in 1843, 454 moved into the new Free Church. Starting with nothing—no manse, no church building—the new Church flourished throughout Scotland as an alternative establishment. Within a year nearly 500 new churches had been built, all financed by private donation. Soon the new Free Church was undertaking an ambitious programme of church, manse, school and college building, setting up numerous mission stations overseas and restructuring Calvinist theology.[97]

Ministers and schoolmasters who broke with the established Church gave up their church buildings, their homes and stipends. Many had large families to support—a family of twelve was not unusual. And if the families suffered, with wives and children becoming seriously ill and even dying as a result of the privations they endured, the parishioners too gave self-sacrificially.

The Free Church went from strength to strength, making inroads into areas, such as Lewis, which had previously clung to the Catholic Church. As well as the Irish mission, the presence of a strong Catholic landowner had been a major contributory cause to the persistence of the older faith, notably in Barra, South Uist and Eriskay, as well as in Lochaber, Moidart and Knoydart—but these links had been weakened with the Clearances.

Robert Murray McCheyne did not live to see the Disruption: he had died of typhus two months before. A friend wrote of him: 'I have sometimes compared him to the silver and graceful ash, with its... leaves of gentle green, reflecting gleams of happy sunshine. The fall of its leaf too, is like the fall of his—it is green tonight, and gone tomorrow—it does not sere, nor whither.'[98]

Religious revival and land reform, 1840s–1880s

Dr Kennedy of Dingwall (quoted in the previous chapter) noted that the great 'spiritual prosperity', the result of religious awakenings in 19th-century Scotland, took place exactly when 'the cruel work of eviction began to lay waste the hillsides and glens of the north'.

Critics of religion claimed that spiritual revivals made people passive in the face of the Clearances. People who expected 'no continuing city' but 'looked for one to come', as the epistle to the Hebrews puts it (13:14), were not inclined to fight for what was theirs on this earth. Some of those people even have seen the enforced emigration as the Lord's way of carrying the Gospel to the New World, this migration thus extending revival-based mission.

Nevertheless, there is a direct link between some revivals within the Free Church and the eventual attempt by Highlanders to gain control of the land. For one thing, sermons by ministers and laymen became a major art form, as did prayers and hymns rooted in the recently translated scriptures, and the powerful idiom of the Gaelic sermon, together with the authority of the minister, helped to strengthen the sense of self-worth of oppressed, marginalized people. Speaking on the sufferings of Christ, for example, Francis Macbean of Corpach, near Fort William, said, 'Cut round the horizon and turn the vault of heaven into a bowl and fill it to the brim. This is but a drop beside the cup that was given him to drink.'

Such images would be discussed at the fireside at home and relayed to family members who had been too frail to make the meetings—or were not yet 'awakened'. Concerned for the souls of the unconverted, folk would doubtless have quoted a saying like the following one from Domhnull na h-Urnaigh (Donald of the prayers): 'The hypocrite's faith is as stout as a straw rope, and can easily be seen, but it will not stand the strain. But the faith of the child of God is of fine gold. It can be drawn as fine as a hair, that can be seen only when the sun shines upon it.'[99]

A feature of Highland Free Church spirituality after the Disruption was the rise of lay preachers and Bible expositors called the 'Men'—not because they were not women, but because they were not ministers. Unlike the Church of Scotland ministers who had been educated in English-speaking Scottish universities and may not even have spoken Gaelic, the Men were local people who were not set apart in lifestyle, work, education or language from the community they served. Many of these people became major leaders in the pressure for land reform and crofters' rights. Those who had led revival in the 1840s also led the campaign for justice in the 1870s and 1880s and won the respect of their congregations, both as spiritual men who knew their scriptures and as key figures in the community who fought to improve the lot of their people. The message of liberation expressed in the scriptures struck deep chords in the hearts and minds of people oppressed by poverty and injustice.

'WHAT FOR DINNA YE TAK A SAIL TO ROME?' IRISH CATHOLICS AND SCOTTISH PRIESTS

Although the national Church of Scotland, formed at the time of the Reformation in 1560, was never uniformly dominant in Scotland, its position was further weakened in the 19th century, not just by the setting up of the Free Church but also by the influx of immigrant Irish to the great industrial centres of Scotland, notably Glasgow, the Clyde basin, Dundee and the mining villages which were developing in the central belt between Edinburgh and Glasgow. This immigration also posed a problem for the Roman Catholic hierarchy, since more priests were needed.

In 1792 it had been reckoned that the number of Catholics in the city of Glasgow could be counted in a few hundreds, and Ayrshire, historically

Presbyterian and Covenanting, could number even fewer. But Father William Thomson, a priest in Ayrshire, estimated that in 1834 (twelve years before the Great Hunger) there were about 6,000 Catholics in the county, a great increase. The Irish were often very poor—and although, like immigrants the world over, families worked hard and tried to better themselves, the influx of so many newcomers raised the spectre of a drain on the Poor Relief funds.

Catholic seminaries had been founded at first in Banffshire, then beside the River Don in Aberdeenshire. Many ordinands were pure Scots speakers, which caused a linguistic difficulty, as a large part of the Irish immigrants spoke only Irish Gaelic—but even those who spoke English would have had a problem with Scots.

When an outspoken priest, Father Andrew Scott, clashed with his Irish flock over finance (what else!) he suggested in Scots that they should all become Presbyterians, or else take the matter up with the Vatican: 'If yer nae pleas't wi' the way I dae fer yer gude, what for dinna ye tak a sail to Rome, and see hoo ye come on at the Vatican, if ye ken whar that is.' (If you're not pleased with the way I'm working for your own good, why don't you sail off to Rome and see how you get on at the Vatican, if you know where that is.')

Father Andrew showed a high degree of contempt and a low level of understanding, especially for the Irish radicals amongst his flock. Nevertheless, he was a devoted pastor who served his people heroically during a cholera epidemic and did much to further the Catholic cause in Glasgow.[100]

Some Irish immigrants came from Belfast and were Protestant, bringing with them the Orange Order, an organization called after William of Orange and set up to defend the Protestant cause. There were inevitably clashes. Extreme Protestant groups produced inflammatory sermons and booklets which derided Catholicism. Catholics tended to form an inward-looking community based on self-help within their parish. Although a few leading figures among the Scottish aristocracy became Catholic and generously gave money, Catholics were mainly centred in poorer housing areas in big cities and remained a working-class minority throughout the 19th century.

However, Catholics and Protestants joined together in Temperance movements; and the 19th century also saw the growth of the Salvation Army, the Band of Hope, Christian Endeavour and the Mission Hall. Less and less could the Scottish church scene be considered monochrome in working-class areas. In newly developing middle-class districts and suburbs, however, the Church of Scotland still held the allegiance of the more affluent and genteel.

'A ST FRANCIS OF ABERDEEN': THE WRITING OF GEORGE MACDONALD

The Congregational Church, Baptists and Independents, and various Mission Halls had spread into Scotland in the wake of the Union of the Parliaments (1707) and the 18th-century revivals, and attracted people who could not identify with the established Church. Some were High-landers who, after the collapse of the Jacobite Uprising, settled into farming or fishing communities along the east coast, many taking the innocuous surnames of Smith or Brown.

One clansman kept his surname in its anglicized form, MacDonald. He settled in Portsoy in Banff (famous for black marble). The family then moved to the historic town of Huntly in Aberdeenshire, where their son George MacDonald was born in 1824.

George MacDonald became a much-admired writer whose novels outsold those of Charles Dickens. His books fell out of mode as the leisurely pace of life which had allowed people to absorb long novels changed, with the advent of the motor car, the silent movie and global warfare. Three children's books, *The Princess and the Goblin*, *The Princess and Curdie* (which had been praised as highly as *Alice in Wonderland*) and *At the Back of the North Wind* continued to make a lasting impression on new readers.

The images of the Princess's fairy godmother, her fire of roses and the vital, invisible fairy gossamer she spun to guide the Princess through the dark underworld of the goblins wove themselves into the readers' imaginations, where they continued to shine as unforgettably as the 'lilies of the field' whose glory surpasses Solomon's. C.S. Lewis summed up the feelings of many when he said that reading MacDonald 'baptized' his imagination. So indebted to MacDonald was Lewis that he wrote, 'I have never concealed the fact that I regarded him as my master; indeed I fancy I have never written a book in which I did not quote from him.'[101]

C.S. Lewis' life-changing discovery of MacDonald's writings rescued the Scottish writer from oblivion and gave him a wide following once more. A generation or so before Lewis, the Catholic apologist, literary critic and writer, G.K. Chesterton, had been equally enthusiastic. 'I... can testify to a book that has made a difference to my whole existence,' he wrote. 'It is called *The Princess and the Goblin* and it is by George MacDonald.'[102]

Perhaps not surprisingly, given his own Catholic beliefs, Chesterton set MacDonald in a literary tradition which bypassed Calvinism and, harking back to the spirit of medieval Scotland, 'represented what Scottish religion should have been':

Now, among the many men of genius Scotland produced in the 19th century, there was only one... who really represented what Scottish religion should have been, if it had continued the colour of the Scottish medieval poetry. In his particular type of literary work he did indeed realize the apparent paradox of a St Francis of Aberdeen, seeing... around every flower or bird... a certain special sense of significance, which the tradition that most values it calls sacramental. To have got back to it, or forward to it, at one bound of boyhood, out of the black Sabbath of a Calvinist town, was a miracle of imagination.[103]

Robert Murray McCheyne and George MacDonald represent two completely opposite expressions of Scottish Christianity. McCheyne sought God in the scriptures; MacDonald, as Chesterton pointed out, saw a sacramental holiness in the whole of creation. The whole issue of Christianity and Scottish culture remains contentious and polarized. We shall explore the dilemma in the last chapter, but there remain three further pieces to be stitched into this 19th-century patchwork: foreign mission, social reform and medical discovery.

'THE FEATHERS FROM THE ANGELS' WINGS': DAVID LIVINGSTONE, MARGARET WILSON AND MARY SLESSOR OF CALABAR

The 19th century was the era of colonialism and of foreign mission. Missionaries braved many dangers and made lasting improvement, particularly in the fields of medicine and education. The reduction of female circumcision in Kenya, the improved status of women and children, the survival of twins, and the education of women and outcasts are particular results of the devoted labours of foreign missionaries. Scotland can boast a host of names: some, like David Livingstone (1813–73), are internationally known; others have long since been forgotten. Perhaps, among the plethora of names, special mention needs to go to missionary wives who bore children far from home and endured privations, sickness and early death for the sake of their calling. An early missionary wife, Margaret Bayne, born in 1795 and nearly nine years older than her husband John Wilson, left home with him to sail to India in 1828. From London she wrote to her sisters:

Much as I felt the pang of separation after parting with you, I did not fully realize its agony till now... and when I think of never seeing you, never again listening to the accents of your voices, I would sink into despair, were I not strengthened by an unseen energy and by the hope of a blessed reunion.

The Wilsons set up home in Bombay, where Margaret, starting from scratch, had within six months established six schools with a total of 120 pupils. She offered hospitality to Christians and Hindus, gave birth to four children, worked with her husband in the church which he founded in 1831, contributed to missionary journals, and prepared textbooks for schools and devotional books for new converts. In addition she fostered abandoned children. 'I have four little girls living in the house,' she wrote to her sisters on 12 May 1834, continuing:

One of them... was found in the bazaar at Jalna. Other two were sold as slaves during the last famine... The fourth is a little half-caste girl, totally destitute. I expect two little girls today, who have been left in very melancholy circumstances. They are the children of European parents. Their father was a medical man, but of no respectability.

In addition, Margaret Wilson taught women to read, visited the poor and destitute and, wrote her husband, 'She ever communicated to me the most valuable counsel, and the most exciting encouragement in my work… Her prayers for the nourishment of the divine life within her soul, and for success in the propagation of the Gospel, prevented the rising sun; and they formed the engagement of many of her midnight hours.' Margaret died in 1835, shortly after the birth of her fourth child. 'To her, more than to any other, is due the rapid progress of female education in Bombay,' was the verdict of the historian.[104]

Some missionaries came from humble origins. David Livingstone worked in weaving sheds at the mill in Blantyre from 7am, attended school in the evening and studied until midnight.

Mary Slessor (1848–1915) endured childhood poverty—her father was an alcoholic. The family moved to Dundee in 1859 and Mary worked as a mill-weaver. She went to West Africa 1876 as a missionary teacher in Calabar, now part of Nigeria. Mary Slessor was very much an individualist. In an age where women missionaries were restricted, Mary worked independently and flouted European customs by going hatless and barefoot. She worked as a reforming chief, and was known as 'The White Queen of Okoyong'. She was made a member of the Order of St John of Jerusalem as well as a British Consular Agent, representing the Crown. She settled tribal disputes, encouraged outside trade, and discouraged ritual killings at funerals and witchcraft trials. But above all, Mary Slessor is remembered for her work in saving twins. The Efik people of Calabar regarded twins as an aberration and allowed only one of the pair to live. Mary Slessor confronted tribal chiefs with total conviction that they were wrong and, happily for the twins, overturned the social order of the tribe. She adopted rejected children and twelve years before her death paid a visit to her native Scotland, bringing four little girls with her. At one point they visited the Border town of Selkirk and were taken to a photographer. As he prepared his camera, the first snow of winter began to fall. The girls rushed to the window and watched, entranced. 'Oh, Ma,' they exclaimed, 'the feathers from the angels' wings.'[105]

Whatever mistakes missionaries may have made, the impact of the gospel they preached, perhaps even more by their actions than their words, fell on the 'field' like 'feathers from angels' wings'.

'WHOEVER WELCOMES A LITTLE CHILD IN MY NAME WELCOMES ME': DR THOMAS GUTHRIE AND RAGGED SCHOOLS

In 1825 Edinburgh was the third largest city in Britain, with a population of 120,000. The elegant New Town was being developed, but within the Old Town conditions were dire. One tenement in the Canongate housed 125 people in 35 rooms. Vaccination had reduced—but not eliminated—the incidence of smallpox. Measles and diphtheria were childhood killers and in 1832 cholera affected 2317 people in Edinburgh and Leith. The mortality rate was 60 per cent. Many ministers and pastors would have comforted the bereaved in the age-old words of Job, 'The Lord gives and the Lord takes away; blessed be the Name of the Lord.' Nevertheless, many clergy worked actively to improve the plight of the poor. One of the ministers most associated with the care of homeless children was Dr Thomas Guthrie (1803–73).

Dr Guthrie joined the Free Church after the Disruption. He was a much-admired preacher whose listeners were totally carried away, so much so that when Dr Guthrie described a disaster at sea in one sermon, a sailor in the congregation jumped up and pulled off his coat, ready to rush to the rescue of the drowning.[106] Like the English philanthropists Dr Barnardo and the Earl of Shaftesbury—who visited the Scots minister to learn from his work—Thomas Guthrie went about the streets in search of children sleeping rough. He set up 'Ragged Schools' in which children were housed and fed and given a basic education and practical training. One centre became an Industrial School where boys were given a technical training. Later the building, dedicated to Dr Guthrie, was used as an Approved School for delinquent boys.

Among the statues arrayed along the south side of Princes Street, the one dedicated to Dr Thomas Guthrie includes a small boy beside the minister in his flowing gown.

SURGERY BECOMES AN ART, AND PAIN IS RELIEVED: JAMES YOUNG SIMPSON AND THE DISCOVERY OF CHLOROFORM

With pain you will give birth to children. (Genesis 3:16)

Not far from Dr Guthrie's statue is one which commemorates James Young Simpson, the pioneer of pain relief. He was born (7 June 1811) the eighth child of a family whose fortunes were at rock bottom. His mother died when James was only nine. He carried the pain of being motherless all his days—but he retained all his mother's intelligence, energy and drive. Generously supported by an elder brother, James graduated as a doctor in 1832, aged 21, and soon became Senior President of the Royal Medical Society. Eight years later he became Professor of Midwifery, the least-esteemed of all branches of medicine at that time.

Married and with a young family, James Young Simpson set up home at 52 Queen Street and began consultations there. His patients included poor women from the wynds and closes of the Old Town as well as aristocratic ladies. On 19 January 1847 Dr Simpson became the first person in Europe ever to use anaesthetic (ether) in childbirth. It is said that the baby delivered with the aid of ether was named Anaesthesia and that one of Dr Simpson's proudest possessions was a photograph of the girl at the age of 17. On the same day he was appointed Physician Accoucher (midwife) to Queen Victoria. Concerned above all about relieving pain, he continued to experiment with drugs in his own home and then in the Royal Infirmary.

Surgery was set to make an enormous leap forward. Up till then, operations had consisted of little more than amputations, the removal of external tumours and tooth extraction, and the death rate was high. But Simpson's use of chloroform met with severe criticism. Colleagues in the medical world disapproved: pain formed character, they said. The Church also disapproved: women should suffer in childbirth, the ministers said, quoting Genesis 3:16. But James correctly argued that the original Hebrew word translated 'pain' actually meant 'burdensome toil'. The matter was finally resolved in favour of pain relief when Simpson's royal patient, Queen Victoria, used chloroform during labour.

James Simpson died in 1870 at the age of 58. He had helped rob surgery of its terrors. The hallmark of his life was compassion and his Christian faith undergirded his whole life. When a journalist once asked what was his greatest discovery, he replied, 'That I have a Saviour.'

Simpson's residence in Queen Street, Simpson House, now belongs to the Church of Scotland where Christian workers offer counselling and support to young people and adults on drugs, pioneering major projects in this field. James Young Simpson is also remembered every time babies delivered safely in Edinburgh's Royal Infirmary grow up to ask where they were born. They are told, 'In the Simpson's'—for the Maternity Hospital is called by the name of the surgeon who did so much to help women in childbirth.[107]

The 19th century debated with much anguish the problem of faith and science. James Young Simpson showed that a person of faith could also pioneer new medical techniques—that faith could support and motivate scientific discovery. In this way, too, he paved the way for the Church of Scotland's active involvement in social services which was to be developed in the next century.

CHAPTER 9

MISSION & CARE IN THE 20TH CENTURY

'Feed My Lambs'

**When they had finished eating, Jesus said to Simon
Peter, 'Simon son of John, do you truly love me? ... Feed
my lambs... take care of my sheep.'**
JOHN 21:15–16

World War I decimated the number of men, young and old, who worked
the farms and crofts and whose craft supported the villages throughout
rural Scotland, while depression and unemployment in the cities also took
their toll on faith.

The interwar years saw many tensions within and between the
Churches. In 1929 the Church of Scotland united with some of the Free
Churches. Some Highland groups, strictly Sabbath-keeping and Gaelic-
speaking, stayed out of the merger. An English-speaking evangelical group
also stayed out of the union and, under Revd James Barr (1862–1949),
formed the United Free Church (UF). UF worship is like the mainstream

Church of Scotland (indeed an outsider wouldn't notice the difference), but the United Free Church has its own General Assembly, supports its own mission and remains determinedly free of any kind of alignment with the State. It was also the first Church to admit women to the ordained ministry. Professor Barr's own daughter, Revd Elizabeth Barr, was for many years Moderator as well as minister, at a time when such a thing was still unthinkable in the Church of Scotland. At least one other talented woman, called to the ordained ministry, moved over into the United Free Church for that very reason.

Depression and high unemployment drew many Christians towards social and political action. It was at this period that George MacLeod, as we saw in Chapter 2, set up the Iona Community. John Wheatley (1869–1930), Irish by birth, Catholic by baptism, socialist by conviction, fought a lonely battle, not least against the clergy of his own Church, who feared anything that hinted at Communism. John Wheatley rose to prominence out of great poverty. He became Minister of Health in the first Labour Government, fighting to better the housing conditions of the poor, yet he was always discriminated against. After enduring a bitter anti-Catholic campaign, Wheatley lost a libel action against the Church of Scotland. Later, Wheatley was told by one of the jurors that when the foreman of the jury had presented his case, he had said, 'Don't forget that he's an Irishman, a Catholic and a Socialist; and our King and Queen are in Edinburgh this week.' Wheatley died soon after, but he had opened the doors into political life for other Catholics to follow.[108]

The 1918 Education Act was a major step forward for the Catholic community in Scotland. The Act brought Catholic schools within the State system and safeguarded Catholic interests. Catholic students could now enter the professions and become involved in public life. Better education and housing resulted in a rising Catholic middle class. But the trend towards integration did not go unattacked. In a situation of high unemployment it was easy to scapegoat the immigrant Irish, and John Wheatley was not alone in enduring discrimination. However, the inter-war period produced a well-educated laity, preparing the way for the ground-breaking decisions of Vatican II (1963). It also produced a saint, a very ordinary young woman from a city slum.

Margaret Sinclair lived in the centre of Old Edinburgh, in Blackfriars Street, leading steeply off the High Street. Thousands of tourists visit Edinburgh each year and many walk the historic Royal Mile. Few realize that at the beginning of the 20th century this area was one of the poorest and least desirable in the whole city. Life was far from easy, but Margaret was seen from her earliest years as being a comfort to the neighbourhood, working a long day as a French polisher (meticulous, tedious work) and in addition visiting sick neighbours with soup or home-made baking, scrubbing their floors and seeing they had enough money for their needs—paying out of her own meagre purse.

Margaret Sinclair died when she was 25. Her life was unremarkable—and yet it was holy. Even as a small child Margaret had found the meaning of the words, 'Hallowed be your Name', and this transformed everything she did and was.

Margaret joined the Order of the Poor Clares when she was only 23. Typically, she did not choose to be an enclosed Sister, but entered upon the much harder life of those who worked in the laundry and kitchen and went out with collecting tins for the needs of the order. Her modesty and reserve meant that she was always underestimated. Just as at school, people felt that there was nothing remarkable about Margaret—except that she never complained, even though her Superior tried to crush her by mocking her 'coarse (Scottish) speech', belittling her and testing her with penances and acts of obedience that were not just humiliating but verged on cruelty. Margaret bore all this patiently, always noticing when others were feeling low and trying to cheer them up. Her prayer was, 'O, my God, help me always to take up your cross cheerfully and follow you.'

Margaret was professed as Sister Mary Francis of the Five Wounds. But almost immediately, the sore throat and cough which had been troubling her were diagnosed as tuberculosis of the throat—and now the hidden life of total self-sacrifice, of giving cheerfully to others and accepting the Lord's will in everything, became noted for what it was. The Sisters who cared for Margaret said, 'She accepted all the sufferings of her last illness with complete joy, for the love of God.' Margaret's path to holiness seems conventional Catholic piety—the peak of Christian commitment was for a girl to 'take the veil' and become a nun. But her spiritual director, putting her forward for sainthood, said that it was what he knew of her life before she became a nun which made her worthy to be called blessed. The virtues he and others stressed were not religious ones, but the quiet, heroic holiness of everyday life which all Christians are called to and which Margaret consistently exemplified.[109]

It was exactly this kind of practical Christianity which Vatican II hoped other Catholics would emulate. The challenge to live for God in simple, ordinary ways became particularly relevant in post-war years as all the mainstream churches lost their dominant position in national life.

'Lt Thomson, God wants you to be an evangelist': D.P. Thomson and home mission

World War I had made the young George MacLeod a pacifist; it made 21-year-old Lieutenant D.P. Thomson an evangelist. The war took him from an apprenticeship with a firm of jute merchants in his native city, Dundee. As a young officer in France and Salonika, he cared for other soldiers spiritually. A New Zealand businessman in Salonika, observing the young officer, laid his hand on D.P.'s shoulder and said, 'Lt Thomson, God wants you to be an evangelist.' This sense of call never left him. The young man who was to become known all over Scotland only by his initials, D.P., was invalided out of the army in 1916. The war had already killed two brothers and five cousins. 'If I had been spared when others were taken,' he wrote, 'it was not just for the resumption of a commercial career.' He immediately launched into action as an evangelist, first as a lay preacher and then as a minister.

If the 19th century had seen the Kirk lose its universal hold on Scottish life, the 20th saw that process continue. D.P.'s long life was given not so much to stemming the outflow from the churches, as bringing an inflow into active faith. He set up Seaside Missions within the Church of Scotland and sent students out on teams. Interested in foreign mission, he nevertheless gave his energies to the setting up of a training centre for evangelism at home. He preached from coast to coast and in 1947 became involved with the Revd Tom Allan of North Kelvinside Church, Glasgow, in a movement called 'Tell Scotland'. Tom Allan later became minister of the Tron Church in Glasgow's city centre. The Tron became a spiritual home for thousands of people. Its doors were open all day and there was always someone inside, as office workers and shoppers alike drew aside to pray. It bore the slogan, 'The Church at the heart of the city with the city at its heart'—and the demands of the city wore the minister out. Tom Allan died of a heart attack at the age of 50. D.P. laboured on, influencing a whole post-war generation of young Christians, ministers and lay people. He went on to found his most famous lay training centre, still in existence in Crieff, dedicated to Scotland's first evangelist, St Ninian.

RUNNING THE RACE: ERIC LIDDELL

If anyone competes as an athlete, he does not receive the victor's crown unless he competes according to the rules. (2 Timothy 2:5)

On one occasion, D.P. Thomson invited an outstanding amateur athlete, Eric Liddell (1902–45), to preach. Liddell's father, a missionary in China, was known to D.P. Eric Liddell readily agreed and became a very popular speaker, not so much for his ability to speak, but for his whole lifestyle, which was completely committed to God.

Eric Liddell won the Crabbe Cup as outstanding athlete of the Scottish Amateur Athletic Games four years running, but he reached world fame for the Olympic race he did not run—the 100 yards, his strongest event. The race was scheduled for a Sunday and Eric refused to dishonour the Sabbath day. He was immediately branded as a traitor and the then Prince of Wales tried to persuade him to change his mind. But Eric Liddell stood firm and put his name down for a race he had no hope of winning. The story goes that just as he was about to warm up for the start, an unknown person thrust a piece of paper into his hand. Its message, '1 Samuel 2:30', gave Eric Liddell the encouragement he needed, for he knew his Bible chapter and verse and recognized the reference: 'Those who honour me I will honour.'

Eric Liddell won the gold medal for his country—and gave God the glory. But his mind was set on foreign mission and he soon sailed for China, where he was ordained in 1932. Eric married—but sent his wife and children abroad as conditions in China worsened with the outbreak of war. Eric was interned, and now, the man who had refused to run on a Sunday for his own glory set all his principles aside for the sake of young people who had no other day in which to take part in sports, and used his Sundays behind prison bars to help them train and race.

Eric Liddell died from a brain tumour shortly before liberation in 1945. He had fought against blackness and self-doubt caused by the ravages of cancer in his brain. In so doing, he ran perhaps the hardest race in his life for the prize, knowing, as the apostle Paul put it, 'Now there is in store for me the crown of righteousness, which the Lord, the righteous Judge, will award me on that day' (2 Timothy 4:8).

'FEAR NOT, FOR I HAVE REDEEMED YOU': REVD DONALD CASKIE OF THE SCOTS KIRK IN PARIS

He knows the way I take. (Job 23:10)

Donald Caskie, an Islayman and a native Gaelic speaker, fluent also in French, became minister of the Scots Kirk in Paris just before the war. The following account of his experiences comes from his book *The Tartan Pimpernel*, (Oldbourne, 1957). Bible quotes are from the Authorized Version.

Forced by the German invasion of France to close his church, Donald joined the flow of refugees to the coast, reaching Bordeaux to learn that the last ship, crowded with refugees, had been torpedoed. The German armies were only a few hours' march away. Exhausted and dispirited, Donald Caskie opened his Bible at random. He found the book of Job: 'I shall go forward, but he is not there, and backward, but I cannot perceive him... But he knoweth the way I take.'

In unexpected ways and through unexpected people the Scots padre found himself guided to Marseilles. He wrote:

We Highlanders have the gift of second sight which admits us to dimensions of the unseen world... As I knelt in that house in Marseilles all things became clear. The city outside the window was remote. Its noises diminished and I was secure in the embrace of God. My new vocation came with the clarity of crystal. The words of the Prophet Isaiah sounded in my ears, 'And thine ears shall hear a word behind thee saying: this is the way, walk ye in it... Comfort ye, comfort ye my people... Feed the hungry, clothe the naked, bring deliverance, and the opening of the prison to them that are bound. That is your task. Arise and go.'

Immediately I rose from my knees. Instinctively I looked around the room. I had heard the Voice so clearly that I thought I should surely see someone... I heard an English voice. 'Padre, we've been looking for you... We need you to help starving soldiers and airmen from Dunkirk.'

The commission was the beginning of Donald's involvement with the French Underground. Through hair-raising experiences and many miracles, he fed and sheltered Allied servicemen and set them on their dangerous way across the Pyrenees into Spain. In the end he was betrayed, arrested and put into solitary confinement. On the walls of his cell, with a thumbnail which had grown as long as a hook, Donald inscribed his name, and his rank as Church of Scotland pastor. Then he scratched the words: 'Thus saith the Lord... Fear not, for I have redeemed thee, I have called thee by name, thou art mine. When thou passeth through the waters I will be with thee; and through the rivers, they shall not overflow thee. When thou walketh through the fire, thou shalt not be burned, neither shall the flame kindle upon thee...'. Later he learnt that those words, scratched so laboriously in the darkness, had saved the life of another prisoner:

More than a month passed before I saw a human being apart from the silent guard. The dungeon I made a world of memory and prayer. For hours I continued to receive the Scriptures. Whole days would pass while in reverie I reconstructed my past life... I would see again the Paps of Jura, the view across the water, the blue hills and green fields, the lapping water on the beach... On the Sundays I devised for myself, I projected my soul to Islay and the mid-morning Gaelic service when the blessed words are spoken in our native language... So I lived out my solitary days filling the dungeon with the laughter of my family and friends until the day came when the dungeon door opened and a figure was hurtled through to fall beside me. Almost timorously I touched him and then helped him to his feet.

The new prisoner had undergone such torments at the hands of the Gestapo that, back in his cell, he had been on the point of cutting a vein and killing himself. But just at that moment he had looked up and seen the words from Isaiah Donald had written with his thumbnail. They comforted him and saved his life.

Donald was sentenced to death. He asked to see a chaplain—and the German chaplain, Helmut Peters, eventually saved the Scots minister's life.

With wonderful tenderness he raised his hands and looked at me, a long gravely gentle look on his face. 'Ah, yes. There are opposing camps and God has placed us, one in each, but the link that binds us, my dear friend, is closer than the tie my nation has on me or yours on you. The cross indeed is the symbol of our common faith.'

So, thanks to the intervention of his brother in faith, Donald Caskie lived to take his part in the rebuilding of the Scots Kirk. On 10 April 1957 Queen Elizabeth came to Paris to lay the foundation stone.

JANE HAINING, MATRON OF THE GIRLS' HOME, VOROSMARTY UTCA, BUDAPEST

Do you truly love me...? Feed my lambs. (John 21:15)

Donald Caskie survived the war. A Scottish woman in Budapest, Jane Haining from Ayrshire, did not. Instead, she became the only Scots woman to die in Auschwitz concentration camp.

Jane Haining was born at Lochendhead Farm, Dunscore, Ayrshire on 6 June 1897. After a brilliant school career—she won 46 prizes—Jane turned down the chance to go to university. Instead, in autumn 1915, Jane left home to go to Glasgow where she completed a course in business studies, and started work in J&P Coates, thread manufacturers in Paisley. She joined Queen's Park West Church and became a Sunday School teacher. In 1927, Jane heard about the Church of Scotland Mission amongst the Jewish community in Hungary and told a friend, 'I have found my life's work!' Thereupon she did a course in the Glasgow School of Domestic Science, responded to an advertisement for the job of matron in the Girls' Home of the Kirk's Jewish Mission school in Budapest and on 20 June 1932, 'a fresh sunny morning with the promise of heat in it', she set out for Budapest.

Many of the girls at the home came from elite families, but even so, some were the casualties of family breakdown, and all were victims of growing restrictions and overt anti-Semitism in Hungary. Jane wrote:

Just last night I had a long talk with one of my children who finishes with us this year. She is a little unwanted one of Jewish blood who was adopted and brought up by a Christian family. The child has always been taught to look upon her foster parents as her real parents and did not know otherwise. Her longing was to be a teacher, but in the eyes of the law she is Jewish and may not be a teacher, so she had to be told the truth. Of course it was bitter to swallow.

Some of the girls needed a lot of mothering. Jane wrote in 1937, 'We have one nice little mite who is an orphan and is coming to school for the first time. She seems to be a lonely wee soul and to need lots and lots of love, so we shall see what we can do to make life a little happier for her.'

As hatred of Jews increased, refugee children began to appear in the home. Jane wrote, 'What a ghastly feeling it must be to know that no one wants you and to feel that your neighbours literally grudge you your daily bread.'

As the noose tightened about the Jews of Europe, the Scots Mission under the protection of the Swedish Red Cross sheltered mothers and children, hid fathers and helped people stay out of the ghetto by issuing false documents. Then, on 19 March 1944, the Nazis took possession of Budapest.

Three weeks later, the Gestapo arrested Jane Haining. Jane had been denounced by the school cook's son-in-law, whom she had confronted when she found him helping himself to food supplies intended for the girls.

Flimsy charges were brought against her: she had worked among Jews and wept when the girls had attended class wearing yellow stars; she had dismissed her non-Jewish housekeeper; she had listened to the BBC news, had British visitors, had visited British prisoners of war and sent them parcels, and she had been active in politics.

Jane admitted all the charges except the last. She was transferred to a prison camp outside Budapest. Then, on 12 May, she was crammed into a cattle wagon with 90 other prisoners and transported to Auschwitz, where she was tattooed with the number 79467.

The grim prison camp is set in peaceful countryside. Hills smudge the horizon and Jane, like the psalmist of old, found comfort from 'the strength of the hills'. Her last letter ends, 'There is not much to report from here. Even here on the way to Heaven are mountains, but further away than ours. I send appropriate greetings to the whole family and kiss and embrace you.' It was dated 15 July 1944. It was postmarked Auschwitz, 21.7.44—and by that time Jane was dead. The letter, like the others Jane sent, doesn't speak of her own sufferings, but simply voices her concern for her friends.

Jane Haining is honoured in her own church in Glasgow by two memorial windows. The Jewish community in Budapest have also erected a commemorative plaque in the former Mission building, which now houses a State school, the Vorosmarty School. The Presbyterian Church, dedicated to St Columba, still meets within the same building and two memorials to Jane Haining have been unveiled there.

But perhaps the memorial she would prefer is the Jane Haining Prize, funded by the Church of Scotland and linked with her home church, Queen's Park. Two Hungarian 14-year-old prize-winners go to Scotland for a week. They meet families from Queen's Park Church and visit Lochenhead Farm, birthplace and childhood home of Jane Haining.

It has been said of Jane Haining that 'among the daughters of Israel she became a mother in Israel, and in the worst day of Israel's suffering, she suffered too'. After her death, a letter arrived from Hungary. It was written by a girl called Anna, Jane Haining's god-daughter. It is perhaps the best epitaph of all.

Suddenly I heard a nice voice, 'O you would be our little Anna.' I could not see anything except a couple of beautiful blue eyes and I felt a motherly kiss on my cheek. So this was my first meeting with Miss Haining and from this very moment I loved her with all my heart... Then she was taken away. I still feel the tears in my eyes and hear in my ears the siren of the Gestapo motor-car. I see the smile on her face while she bade farewell... I never saw Miss Haining again and when I went to the Scottish Mission to ask the minister about her, I was told she had died. I realised she had died for me and for others. The body of Miss Haining is dead, but she is still alive, because her smile, voice, face are still in my heart. I will never forget Miss Haining and I will try to follow in her footsteps.[110]

IN SEASON AND OUT OF SEASON: TWO GREAT BIBLE TEACHERS, WILLIAM BARCLAY AND WILLIAM STILL

Preach the Word; be prepared in season and out of season; correct, rebuke and encourage—with great patience and careful instruction. (2 Timothy 4:2)

William Barclay (1907–78) had studied at the feet of major German theologians, but for all that, he chose a parish on industrial Clydeside. There, his great gift of communication made the gospel available to the 'plain man'. After the war, he used these gifts to bring straightforward Bible teaching into the nation's front rooms via a highly popular Sunday evening television series. Equally popular was his *Study Bible* series, which was translated into many languages, including Estonian and Burmese, and brought a vast correspondence, much of it from countries closed to the gospel.

Television came to Scotland in the 1950s, in time for the coronation of Queen Elizabeth in 1953. The increasing availability of television in the post-war years certainly took people from church, but William Barclay showed that a medium denounced by many ministers of the time could be used to bring Christian teaching to a wide audience. Another minister, Revd William Still (1911–98), sought to make the pulpit a focus of challenging preaching and teaching. 'Willie' Still served as a minister at Gilcomston South Church in Aberdeen from 1945 until his death, never seeking to move on, and never seeking retirement. He remained unmarried but his spiritual children were numerous as he encouraged the resurgence of Evangelicalism. Younger ministers, inspired by his Bible exposition, moved out to 'unstarch', as he would have put it, churches which had grown formal and cold.

The 1950s saw Britain becoming generally more affluent but it was still a time when Scotland observed the Sabbath (Sunday). Shops were shut, bus services curtailed. Christmas Day was not a public holiday. Hogmanay (31 December) and Ne'erday (New Year's Day) were the time when families got together with gifts. Many churches and Mission Halls held Watch Night Services at New Year, and this practice of keeping vigil with prayer and hymn and sermon was gradually extended to include Christmas Eve. The 1950s and 1960s were times when church halls were fully used, even if church attendance on Sundays was beginning to drop. Uniformed youth groups, like Scouts, Guides and the Boys' Brigade, badminton clubs, drama groups and women's guilds all kept the halls' conveners busy. Evangelical churches had midweek gatherings of a more Bible-centred nature—missionary prayer groups, Bible Study for the church members, Christian Endeavour and Band of Hope for youngsters. It was a time when young men carried big black Bibles to open-air meetings on street corners—and a crowd always gathered. 'It's better felt than tellt' ('better to feel it than talk about it'), the evangelists would assure their listeners in homely Scots.

But life was changing. Redevelopment altered the face of many Scottish cities. New towns sprang up, with new challenges to all the churches to provide support for people uprooted from their old neighbourhoods. Churches which had been busy and active in the old downtown areas went into decline: local people moved out and a whole influx of families from the Punjab and Bangladesh moved in. Many opened corner shops. Many more served on the buses. A major controversy took place in the

1960s when a Sikh bus conductor turned up to work dressed in the correct uniform but with a turban instead of the regulation peaked hat. He was dismissed, but the matter was taken up by the press and by city councillors and he was reinstated with his turban. The seeds of cultural and religious pluralism were being sown.

Statistics point to falling church membership. In 1984, 44 per cent of all adult church attenders were Roman Catholic. The Church of Scotland came next with 40 per cent and the other churches mustered only 16 per cent.[111] The numbers have dropped even more since then.

Despite falling church attendance, Christian churches continue to provide social care, supplementing statutory services. The Church of Scotland, for example, is the second biggest care provider in Scotland after the government, and the only one which works on a nationwide basis. The Board of Social Responsibility cares for over 4,000 people, irrespective of religious affiliation. The aim is to keep one step ahead of need in all aspects of care, from dementia in the elderly to drug addiction among children, from provision for the homeless to care for refugees and prisoners. The new millennium has brought challenges to Scottish Christians to work out the implications of Christ's message of faith, hope and love in a world of widening social differences, pluralism, new technological possibilities and a vibrant and self-confident cultural scene. To this we shall turn in our final chapter.

CHAPTER 10

LOST FOR WORDS

In the beginning was the Word.

JOHN 1:1

At the far side of the sea (poetically speaking) is silence. 'Deep calleth unto deep' and the heart attends and is enlarged. This is the great mystery of prayer. It may be that as the churches of the West, and not least of Scotland, enter the third millennium since the birth of Christ, they are called not to sound but to silence. We stand in the desert of declining numbers amidst buildings whose doors are shut. The wind blows where it will, we hear the sound, we trace its path across waving grass or tossing sea, but we cannot control it, despite our attempts to harness its power. An Irish legend says that once Prince Conn-eda (after whom the region of Connaught is called) had defeated evil, he planted three golden apples in his garden. A great tree sprang up which caused the whole realm to produce fruit in abundance. But the unseen, mysterious work of faith is even more subversive than the golden apples of myth.

Generally, it has to do with a readiness to meet people where they are as well as a willingness to take risks. Many city centre churches open their doors to the homeless and the users of the psychiatric services, offering drop-in centres, counselling, coffee and ash-trays. Others provide an alternative way of shopping by using their premises for One World shops, Christian crafts, books and so on.

In Chapter 3 we saw how a church grew up around the healing well linked with St Triduana. That building was destroyed at the Reformation and laid waste, but was rebuilt in the 19th century and dedicated to St Margaret. As the first year of the 21st century was coming to an end, local children vandalized the building, setting it on fire. The ancient crypt and well have survived and out of the loss has come a sense of solidarity. People who don't go to church but were married there or had their babies baptized there have expressed their concern and support. St Margaret's, a growing congregation, has become a centre for community-based care.

At this point in the book I am going to write more personally and share my own concerns. I now live in Poland and this has a bearing on this chapter, but I used to live in Leith, the Edinburgh district next to the area of Triduana's well, and I had heard a lot about St Margaret's. I want to use this Church of Scotland congregation, with its ancient history, as one example of contemporary Scottish Christianity in a local scene. Believing that even if people do not go to church they are on a spiritual journey, St Margaret's congregation taps into the needs of the working-class community through projects which in turn feed the life and worship of the church and have been a catalyst for growth. The various projects aim to improve the quality of life in the area by helping people to help themselves. The minister, Revd Euan Aitken (following in the footsteps of the Iona-inspired minister, Geoff Shaw), serves as a local councillor, bringing theology to bear on the difficulties of life. One particular issue he has raised is the high suicide rate among young men. Pressured by the need to achieve, depressed by unemployment or their sense of inadequacy, young men (who tend to be missing from the average church) need a helpline and support.

The church's over-arching scheme, the Ripple Project, has engendered a lunch club for the elderly, as well as after-school and pre-school care. A single parent voiced the feelings of many when she said, 'This is a God-send. I've been able to train and get a job, which I could never have done otherwise.' She was grateful for a place where she could send her children at a cheap rate and know that they received good-quality care. The church recognizes local needs and asks, 'How can we walk with you?' This is not preaching from the pulpit, but faith worked out in the nitty-gritty of daily life. The projects are born within the congregation, are launched at the Sunday worship and prayed for. People alienated from formal church have seen the value of such service and say, 'This is Christianity as I understand it.'

I personally feel that participatory worship which feeds—and is fed by—the local community is the way forward for churches of every denomination. But those who worship should also be aware of history and tradition. From living in Russia I have learnt the value of tradition and also the value of simple prayer: of lighting a candle, looking at a picture, listening to music—on weekdays as well as Sundays. I was delighted to discover that St Margaret's church is opened during weekdays for two hours a day for people to drop in and pray.

In Russia, people remember the dead at special services. This helps them through the bereavement process. In Poland, too, graveyards are well tended. People visit their family's graves on special occasions, and especially at the Feast of All Souls (2 November), to light candles and remember the dead.

All Souls is preceded by All Saints. The day before that, at Hallowe'en (31 October), Scottish children traditionally go round the doors 'guising'. They dress up and are supposed to sing or recite a poem and receive sweets, an orange and so on. Nowadays they expect money and the song has dwindled to a perfunctory verse. Many Christians feel increasingly unhappy with the emphasis placed on witches at Hallowe'en, both in school and commercially. They also feel distressed at the bare fifteen minutes allowed for a funeral in a crematorium. St Margaret's holds a service for the bereaved each Hallowe'en, the traditional time for remembering the dead. A large number attend—and not only the recently bereaved. Many people who have failed to mourn their loved ones find the burden of loss lifted even years after the event within the prayerful setting of a communal act of remembrance. Tears are shed—and people leave, comforted.

The example of St Margaret's gave me hope for the future. A church with open doors has an open purse—and an open heart. If more churches—and especially ministers—could open their doors and fit into the community, making themselves weak and vulnerable instead of claiming to have all the answers, I am sure the Church of Scotland would grow in numbers and in relevance.

I found the same openness of approach in the Scottish Episcopal Church. Instead of being hierarchical and heavily clergy-based, the Scottish Episcopal Church is looking towards patterns of shared ministry, with the local congregation accepting responsibility for its own life, owning and facilitating the gifts of its membership. Always a minority church in Scotland and very much linked in the past with the gentry— and the Jacobites—the ethos of the Episcopal Church has changed as more people have moved from south of the Border into Scotland—and particularly into the Highlands. Small congregations in remote areas have had to become self-supporting and the Church has developed a scheme of collaborative ministry which, born of economic necessity, in fact fits in with the ethos of the Scottish Parliament which aims at being inclusive and close to people.

Ancient Christian traditions are found to carry new meaning in the new Scotland. St Andrew's bones were brought to Scotland in the misty realm of legend. He became Scotland's patron saint: the first recorded mention of this is in the Declaration of Arbroath in 1320. Significantly, the writers of this great cry for freedom call the apostle 'the gentle Andrew' and it is this very aspect of gentleness and peace which is being brought to the fore today.

St Andrew is said to have been crucified on an X-shaped cross. He appears on a cross in this form on the Great Seal of Scotland in 1286. The white cross on a blue background, known as the saltire, became Scotland's flag. Legend has it that the Scots prayed to Saint Andrew before a battle against the Danes. They looked up and saw the saltire cross etched among the silver stars. It is certainly known that both Wallace and Bruce looked to the Galilean fisherman for protection in battle.

An ancient *Life of St Andrew*, written around the second century and virtually ignored for over a thousand years, has been rediscovered and its various fragments have been pieced together. According to this *Life*, Andrew went to his death for supporting a woman convert who refused to sleep with her pagan husband, having found a new Lover, Christ. Andrew is also said to have persuaded Roman soldiers to disarm. Alastair McIntosh, Fellow of the Centre for Human Ecology in Edinburgh, told *The Times* on the eve of Scotland's national feast, St Andrew's Day (30 November): 'Myths shed light on a nation's soul. They carry the values stitched to the fabric of nationhood... The Saltire symbolizes values including non-violence and feminism.' And he concludes, 'Members of the Scottish Parliament might remember (this) as they gather to govern beneath a flag of which we can be radically proud.'[112]

SCOTLAND'S FIRST MINISTER VISITS THE VATICAN

In 1999 James McMillan, a leading Scottish composer, told newspapers that Catholics (though not himself personally) had been belittled and discriminated against. McMillan was referring to the fact that as young Roman Catholics received higher education in the post-war years and climbed out of the old working-class ghettos, many found themselves set aside at job interviews because they had been to St Patrick's or St Mungo's and not to the local (non-Catholic) senior school—a kind of unwritten closed-doors policy which had been enshrined in years of anti-Catholic prejudice. Further clashes occurred the following year, when Scotland's Labour Government voted to withdraw Section 28 of the Education Act. Cardinal Thomas Winning led a bitter campaign against the Scottish Executive, claiming that this would teach children that homosexuality is a 'normal' lifestyle. But a major breakthrough came when Scotland's First Minister, Henry McLeish, made a historic visit to the Vatican and was granted an audience with Pope John Paul II in November 2000. Cardinal Winning, who was also present at the audience, told reporters that the Pope had spoken of Scotland's 'glorious inheritance', while Mr McLeish told journalists that the Scottish Catholic Church has an absolute right to speak out on matters of conscience, that he valued the contribution of the churches to Scotland and that he hoped the Scottish Parliament would always listen to their voice.[113]

The visit of Scotland's First Minister marked the fourth centenary of the founding of the Scots College in Rome. Born in repression when it was impossible to receive a Catholic education in Scotland, the College supplied priests who went at the risk of their lives to Scotland, later training clergy such as Cardinal Winning himself. The College is a valued Scottish presence in Rome and the First Minister's visit to the Vatican not only redressed years of suspicion and active discrimination against Catholics, it also showed Scotland seriously seeking to strengthen its ties with Europe.

This is good because in the global 'village' we are multi-cultural, multi-faith and multi-language. We have to get on with our neighbours, to celebrate and respect our differences. Citizens of Scotland today speak Punjabi and Cantonese, Mandarin and Arabic, Hindi and Urdu, Gujurati and Lithuanian, Italian and Polish, as well as English, Scots and Gaelic. We must welcome this diversity and learn to live in community. We have seen that a thousand years ago Stephen of Hungary valued the cultural riches a mixture of populations brings to a country. 'A country of one language and one culture is weak and fallible,' he told his son. But diversity brings challenge: churches and individual Christians must think about the cultural context of both worship and language.

Living as an English-speaking foreigner in Poland, I recognize a major concern that English—even if it is merely computer-speak—is becoming a world language, overriding local words in local languages. This is a challenge that few churches in the British Isles address. In the earliest days there were varieties of Celtic spoken in the British Isles. We saw that the Pictish language died, with the result that the astounding stone-carvings—unique, as we said, in Europe—remain a mystery to us. We saw that Irish Columba preached the gospel to the Picts by means of an interpreter. Suppose he had preached in Pictish? Would the language have lasted longer, and does it matter? Does it matter either what language was used, so long as the gospel was preached?

We protect endangered species in the bird, animal and plant world. Should we not also be stewards of language?

'The word lost in the Word': towards a 'theology of language'

And the Word became flesh and dwelt among us. (John 1:14, NKJV)

The Word became one of us and all our little words were subsumed into the Word which created cosmos from chaos. Therefore Christians of every tongue should have a high view of language. Familiarity breeds contempt. We have used words since we were two, we began to commit them to writing when we were about five and therefore we do not value language. There is urban theology, feminist theology, a theology of the environment and 'green' issues, but there is no theology of language. In 1983 a landmark occurred with the translation of the New Testament into Scots by William Lorimer. The Lorimer translation, scholarly and lyrical as it is, is accused of being too literary and too late; none the less, many Scottish Christians concede that the Scots words bring a new excitement and a sense of deep recognition to the scriptures. Yet although many people still speak a form of Scots—and understand better than they can read—the language of the pulpit, of the scriptures and the songs is English, and this is not felt to be an issue.

The same goes for Gaelic. The decreasing number of Gaelic-speaking candidates for the ministry, and the decline of Gaelic-speaking young people, mean that in many places Gaelic preaching has become a thing of the past. Yet although more and more people go to night-classes and courses to study Gaelic and find great pleasure and personal meaning in it, the Highland churches retain a largely defensive attitude to these 'outsiders', ignoring a potential mission-field on their own doorsteps.

Are we not stewards of the languages we speak?

Now the whole world had one language and a common speech... The Lord said, '...Come, let us go down and confuse their language so they will not understand each other.' (Genesis 11:1, 6–7)

Dominance by one language is ultimately an impoverishment. As English and other major languages take over, depth and complexity of expression are replaced by a means of communication which is functional, primitive and bare.

'If the grand piano swallows all the other instruments in the orchestra what will become of symphonies?' asks Fearghus MacFhionnlaigh in an article called 'Creative Tensions: Personal reflections of an Evangelical Christian and Gaelic poet'. MacFhionnlaigh, a Christian poet who has chosen to write in Gaelic, argues that the multiplicity of languages is not a problem. It is a monopolistic world language which is the curse. His article continues:

My burden is that God has delivered humanity from the thraldom of Babel by giving us many languages. The single language was the curse—the multiplicity of languages was the blessing… Are we not stewards also of the languages we speak? … Are we not stewards in particular of the languages unique to our own nations? And if the saying 'It is not the healthy but the sick who need the doctor' holds good culturally also, then where should the attentions of the linguistically-called Scot be? … One of those beams of light from Babel is called Scottish Gaelic. It is flickering and fading. It was in our stewardship but we have neglected it. If it goes out, there will be one less route of escape for mankind. One less window through which to look for and find God. Let us act. Before the light fails. Before the wisdom dies. Before the silence steps closer.[114]

In a conversation with Fearghus MacFhionnlaigh, he told me:

When a work of art or a building is threatened, people campaign, raise funds, care. Language has a long way to go before it receives this sort of attention. All languages, however, are potential avenues for explanation for any of us, so the survival of any one language is a human problem. If you're a Christian and you're called to language, could you do better than by helping out smaller languages? After all, this is a call from God—and God is a God of resurrection.

That is a note of hope for Christians who care about language. I have also found it hopeful to compare the situation of Scotland with other countries in Europe.

Many people visit the most northerly major city in Europe, St Petersburg, but few realize that when Peter the Great founded this model European city in 1703, he did so in marshes inhabited by Finnish-speaking Ingrian people. For a long time the Ingrian people co-existed peacefully with their Slavonic neighbours. However, their fate eventually turned out to be as tragic as that of the Gaelic-speaking people of Scotland. Forcibly deported by Stalin in the 1930s and then again in 1941, to the far, frozen edges of the Soviet Union with terrible loss of life and suffering, their language was silenced. But now they are reviving their churches and their language. It has to be said that the affluent life in Finland contrasts very attractively nowadays with the chaos of a Russia in which their parents and grandparents suffered so much, and presents a juicy carrot towards mastering the difficult language of Finnish. This fact makes the situation of present-day Ingrian people very different from the Gaels of Scotland.

Finland itself, like Scotland, is a small country of five million. In spite of the fact that it has been overrun by powerful neighbours and that Swedish is a compulsory learned language for many Finns, Finland has managed to retain its complex, non-European language. Estonia, Latvia and Lithuania are all small countries which have managed to retain their national languages under major pressures. Poland was wiped off the map of Europe for 150 years, but it has retained its culture and national identity because it did not lose its language.

Nearer to home, Norway, another country of five million, has formed a composite language from several dialects and called it New Norse. This language exists alongside Bokmal, derived from Danish. We ask: why could Scotland, also a country of five million, not also form a composite language out of the various dialects of Scots, and then become bi-lingual with Gaelic? And why could the churches of Scotland not be actively engaged in using all the languages of Scotland? This can only happen when we understand the stewardship as well as the theology of language. It has been said that language is the lifeblood of a nation. When the nation dies, the language becomes artificial and a once-vibrant culture becomes packaged as folklore. So it is vital to preserve language—but to do so, we must preserve its culture.

Because there is no sense of culture or of context, there is no sense of loss when we visit the Highlands and Islands and see roofless houses, empty glens and hills. We listen for the sound of Gaelic and hear only the accents of the southern English.

That is why I raised the question, 'Where are the Gaelic speakers?'

The past is full of complexity, and history is written by the victors. But on the Continent, now that the Iron Curtain has crumbled, Europe has been forced to come to terms with its wartime past, its Holocaust, its ethnic cleansing. Many people make serious acts of forgiveness and reparation and, acknowledging guilt, move forward. I should like to see those who have found comfort in popular 'Celtic'-inspired prayers acknowledge the Highland holocaust. I should like to see words of contrition for the way in which English-speaking Christians have despised Gaelic (and Welsh) and evicted the people from the Highlands and Hebrides. And I suggest that pilgrimages should include the emptied valleys and hillsides whose inhabitants were displaced for deer and sheep. Let pilgrims listen to the silence—understand its source, ponder the meaning of loss and absence, and ponder the tyranny of wealth and a single, dominant culture and language.

'HE'LL TAK' ME GENTLY BY THE HAND DOON BY THE BURNIE SIDE'

The task is daunting, but the challenge must be faced as Scotland moves into the 21st century. The psalms of David have undergirded the Scottish Christian story, giving 'the strength of the hills' to the pilgrim. The best-loved is the 23rd, sung to the tune Crimond. Mr G.A. Watt of Ballantrae, Ayrshire, has sent me a version of Psalm 23. I shall end this exploration of Scottish Christianity with the shepherd-king's words in Scots.

> *I ken my Lord and Shepherd will*
> *A' needfu' things provide:*
> *He'll tak me gently by the hand*
> *Doon by the burnie side.*

Frae thorns and briers he'll keep me free,
But should I gang astray,
He'll pu' me canny wi' his crook
Back tae the narrow way.

When I pass thro' Daith's murky glen,
Of nocht I'll be afraid;
His staff uphauds my faltering feet,
My bield shall be his plaid.

Sure is my food and raiment too,
In spite o' ragin foes;
Sweet scented ile anoints my heid,
My cogie aye o'erflows.

For sure God's mercy shall extend
Through oot ma length o' days,
Sae will I dwell within his hoose
And sing my Shepherd's praise.[115]

Appendix

Chapter 1: The far side of the sea

Here are a few more words of explanation about the Celts. The Latin name 'Gaul' corresponds with the Greek word 'Galatia'—thus tenuously linking 'Celtic' tribespeople and farmers with the Galatians, to whom Paul wrote his epistle.

The term 'Celtic' denotes both language and culture; and people speaking Celtic languages were to be found within and far beyond the islands of Britain and Ireland. A region in south-eastern Poland, now part of Ukraine, was called Galicija, and there is also Galicia in northern Spain. Visitors to northern Portugal can still see the remains of an extensive Celtic settlement called Citania dos Briteiros (the citadel of the Britons). All over central Europe, including the Czech Republic and Austria, parts of France, Germany and Spain, as well as in the British Isles and Ireland, archaeology has revealed splendid works of art—shields, sword hilts, brooches, rings of bronze and gold, jewellery of all kinds, richly carved with flowing spirals and intricate interlace. This art, 500 years before the birth of Christ, bears witness to people who loved adornment and used it lavishly.

The earliest Irish and British epic poems praise a warrior caste: an agricultural society whose serfs harvested wheat and barley and ground meal between rounded stones for bread. The idea of great migrations of people has gone out of favour with archaeologists, who now think in terms of social contact leading to local innovation. Deep in prehistory, around 4500BC, hunters and food gatherers in Ireland first began to sow and harvest corn. A thousand years later, as the earliest pyramid was being built in Egypt, the first corn was sown in the Orkney Islands. Language was linked with new developments: preparing the ground, sowing the seed and harvesting the corn needed words.

CHAPTER 2: COLUMBA & IONA

Some additional material from Adamnan's *Life* shows how pagan practice still mingled with Christian belief. A Christian slave belonging to King Bruide's formidable foster-father, the druid Briochan, was a woman of Columba's own race. In a characteristic example of his support for his own tribe—but also of his care for the powerless against the mighty—Columba thundered that the Pictish prince would die unless he set the slave free. Druid Briochan 'very cruelly and obstinately' refused—and immediately fell mortally ill. However, the king hastily sent messengers to Columba, saying that his foster-father had now agreed to set his slave free, whereupon Columba sent a small white stone to the stricken druid. This stone, he predicted, would be used by God to 'effect the cure of many diseases among this heathen nation'. Indeed, Briochan was healed and the slave was freed—and once again we see how paganism and Christianity were intermingled in Columba's story.

CHAPTER 3: PICTLAND, TRIDUANA & RESTALRIG CHURCH

Here is some more information about Pictish stones. The courtly class—clerics, monks and nobles—are uniquely displayed on Christian stones in Pictland: they are not found on the stone-carvings of Argyll and Northumberland. They show that adornment was linked with prestige. On a tidal island, the Brough of Birsay in Orkney, for example, the foundations of Pictish houses are still visible beside the ruins of Norse buildings. The Brough of Birsay was a major Pictish settlement which yielded a carved stone across which walk depictions of three men. All carry square shields, spears and swords. They wear long robes, but the leader stands out: he wears a crown, his hair is longer and curled, his shield is ornately carved and his robe has extra fronds and weaving at the hem—a totally unique portrayal of a people who left so little in writing, so much in stone.

CHAPTER 4: MEDIEVAL SCOTLAND FROM MARGARET TO MARY

When the son of Mary, Queen of Scots united the Crowns of Scotland and England in 1603, he became James I of England but VI of Scotland. The previous five James Stewarts were colourful characters and piety took a prominent place among other, less God-focused passions. Here is a brief summary of the James Stewarts of Scotland:

James I (1394–1437) was an accomplished poet and skilled harpist who excelled 'the Highland Scots who are esteemed the best performers on that instrument', as the historian John Mair wrote in 1521. Imprisoned in Windsor Castle, the Scots king glimpsed Lady Joan Beaufort walking in the grounds, fell in love with her and wrote a long poem, a fine example of early medieval Scots, entitled 'The Kingis Qhair'. The love affair finished happily: James was set free and married his lady, bringing her north to Edinburgh. However, James succeeded in alienating his people by cruelty, mismanagement and shady fiscal policies. The king's life ended tragically on 21 February 1437 when rival Scots lords besieged the Dominican friary in Perth to which he had retreated. James escaped into a sewer, where he was discovered and murdered. The unsavoury facts became embellished in the king's favour. The story I was taught at school ran like this: armed men battered at the door of the royal hall and the great wooden bolt burst from its frame. One of the queen's serving girls, Kate Douglas, thrust her arm through the empty sockets and protected her monarch with her own body until, inevitably, the door broke down and she was flung aside with a broken arm. James was murdered and Kate too—but she has gone down in history as Kate Bar-lass. This version of the king's death developed as the Stewart dynasty consolidated its power; but also because the Scots, with ancient Celtic traditions of kingship, at no time approved of regicide.

James II (1430–60) brought glitter and prestige to the Scottish court. Nicknamed 'James of the Fiery Face' because of a birthmark, the young king (who was seven when he was crowned on 25 March 1437) had a great passion for the new technology of the day—siege cannon. One of his wedding presents was a gun called Mons Meg, made for the Duke of Burgundy in 1449. The passion proved fatal at the Siege of Roxburgh in

1460, in the Scottish Borders, when one of the king's own guns burst from its casing and killed him. Mons Meg can still be seen in Edinburgh Castle.

Nine-year-old James III (1460–88), whose reign was linked to St Triduana's church in Restalrig, succeeded his father. His marriage to 12-year-old Margaret of Denmark ended an ancient dispute over payment for the Western Isles and brought Orkney and Shetland finally under Scottish rule. But powerful factions within the Scottish nobility vied against the king, not least when the monarch bestowed earldoms on his male lovers. James III died in battle against his own lords, who had rallied behind his 14-year-old son, James, perhaps one of the most romantic, passionate and pious of the Jameses.

James IV (1488–1513) quickly gained control of rival factions. As well as encouraging the arts, the king undertook major building works in Stirling and Edinburgh, where the king's glittering Renaissance court conversed in six languages and included the virtuoso poet, William Dunbar, and the Augustinian monk Robert Carver (1490—1546), whose rich, polyphonic music fell out of favour at the Reformation but is now being recovered and performed.

James is remembered too for developing the Scottish navy. A large warship, the great Michael, big enough to carry 27 cannons and a crew of 300, was built in 1511 at the port of Newhaven, on the Forth. Originally called The Port of Our Lady of Grace, Newhaven was later famous for fishwives in striped skirts and bare feet, who carried their baskets of herring through the streets of old Edinburgh. The port, with ruins of an old monastery, has been attractively restored and is a fine place for a walk on an evening to watch the sunset behind the silhouette of the road and rail bridges, with the distant peak of Ben Lomond etched against the evening sky.

James IV married Margaret of York in 1503, a match which would mean that one hundred years later their grandson James VI would legitimately unite the thrones of Scotland and England. The bride's journey north took seven weeks and when she arrived in Edinburgh a great tournament was held in jousting grounds below the castle. The site is now a car park but the street name holds the memory: King's Stables Road. The marriage of the Thistle and the Rose is commemorated by the royal prayer book, now in Vienna, in which the initials I and M are intertwined with many pearls. The queen's own lavishly illustrated Book of Hours is now in Paris.

From his coronation at Scone, where early kings of Scotland had traditionally been crowned, James successfully fostered the cult of kingship and increased control of the Crown over the Church. He appointed men of his choice, including his own illegitimate sons, to major posts in the Church. Parish revenues were ploughed into the coffers of cathedrals, collegiate churches and universities. An Act of Parliament of 1471 tried to curb this trend which was leaving local parishes in a parlous state. All this directly influenced the pressure for reform which came to a head in the 16th century.

James' reign ended tragically. Favouring ties with France, he ill-advisedly marched south and engaged in battle on Flodden Field on 9th September 1513. Henry VIII sent troops under the command of the Earl of Surrey to drive back the Scots, and the English force won the day. James fought on foot until he was cut down within a spear's length of the English commander.

Distressed by his complicity in his father's death, James had locked a heavy chain around his waist as a lifelong act of penance. It is said that, on the eve of the battle, James removed this belt at the wish of the lady with whom he spent the night—who turned out to be a spy. Never mind the adultery or the treachery, the impious act alone was sufficient to lead to disaster. And indeed it did. Ten thousand men, the flower of Scotland, including James' talented illegitimate son Alexander, perished on Flodden Field, one of the darkest days in Scottish history. 'The prime of our land lie cauld in the clay,' lamented Jean Elliott in the 18th-century *The Flowers of the Forest*.

James V was one year old when he was made king of Scotland. He managed to free himself from royal tutors when he was fourteen. James followed his father's Francophile policies and the resulting breakdown in Scottish-English relationships led to the king's untimely death on learning of the Scottish defeat at the Battle of Solway Moss in 1542. The medieval Stewart kings all died tragically, as did Mary herself, the last Queen of Scotland. Only James VI, nicknamed 'the wisest fool in Christendom', kept his head on his shoulders and died peacefully in his bed.

Chapter 5: The Reformation

An extract from Mary's last letter to her brother-in-law, the King of France, written in French at 2am on 8 of February 1587, six hours before she was to die, points up some of the characteristics of the queen. Her last thoughts were of her servants:

Monssiuer mon beau frère… Royal brother, having by God's will, for my sins, I think, thrown myself into the power of the Queen my cousin, at whose hands I have suffered much for almost twenty years, I have finally been condemned to death by her and her Estates. I have asked for my papers, which they have taken away, in order that I might make my will, but I have been unable to recover anything of use to me… Tonight, after dinner, I have been advised of my sentence: I am to be executed like a criminal at eight in the morning… The Catholic faith and my God-given right to the English crown are the two issues on which I am condemned, and yet I am not allowed to say that it is for the Catholic religion that I die… The proof of this is that they have taken away my chaplain, and although he is in the building I have not been able to get permission for him to come and hear my confession and give me the Last Sacrament, while they have been most insistent that I receive the consolation and instruction of their minister, brought here for that purpose…

It remains for me to beg Your Most Christian Majesty, my brother-in-law and old ally, who have always protested your love for me, to give proof now of your goodness… in paying my unfortunate servants the wages due them—this is a burden on my conscience that only you can relieve…

Mary's letter was probably delivered to her brother-in-law late in 1587 when her physician managed to make his way to France. The letter was handed over to the Scots College in Paris, a seminary for Scottish Catholics to train as priests. After the French Revolution the College was disbanded. The letter eventually found its way back to Edinburgh, where it lies beneath the city in the vaults of the National Library of Scotland. (This information, together with the text of the letter, is published by the National Library of Scotland.)

CHAPTER 6: FAITH & MASSACRE, EDUCATION & REVIVAL IN 18TH-CENTURY SCOTLAND

Glimpses of Scottish domestic life after the Reformation:

An extract from the diary of Andrew Hay, a householder writing in 1659

This morning after I was ready, I took breakfast, and then took my horse to Edinburgh. I rode all the way alone and truly the Lord was pleased to allow me a blink of communion with himself on the way. I found that the rains had done great harm and hollowed all the highways and broken almost all the mill dams in the country... Thereafter I walked through the parks and saw my son's little pony. I found that my neighbour had beaten his wife, and I had enough ado to reconcile them again. Thereafter I retired myself to my chamber and did read awhile... and did change my private prayer with my wife, hand to hand before we go to bed. (Quoted with thanks to the Biggar Museums Trust, spelling modernized.)

How school teachers made ends meet

Cock fighting on Fasten's Eve (Shrove Tuesday) continued until the end of the 17th century, and the killed cocks became the school teacher's property, together with the shilling each pupil brought for the fight. In return the teacher provided ale for the scholars. When a bird tried to escape, it was tied to a post and killed by stones; the scholars paid a half-penny each throw. This too went to the schoolmaster and was often more than the Kirk Session could afford to pay him.

Another throwback to the old Church calendar benefited the schoolmaster: he was given candles at Candlemas (2 February).

In Paisley in 1705 the teacher was given half a guinea to buy a new hat as an encouragement to be more diligent in his work in the school. The hat would raise his status in the community—only the laird or minister wore the three-cornered hat; everyone else wore blue or black woollen bonnets.

School discipline

Physical punishment as discipline in schools continued well into the second half of the 20th century. The 'strap' or 'belt' was a feature of Scottish school life. Recalcitrant or slow children were 'encouraged' by the threat, 'I'll warm your fingers.' Children who were removed from the classroom for punishment would return to whispers of 'What did you get?' The reply would be 'Six', or 'Two of the belt.' It was an offence to belt a pupil anywhere else but on the outstretched hand—and so the tawse was considered a more enlightened form of corporal punishment than the system of caning in England.

In spite of provision made by the Kirk, many children in Scotland had no chance of an education until well into the 19th century. Little boys as young as four were sent naked into chimneys as human brushes. The few who lived into their teens were completely crippled. Miners were thirled (enslaved) to the owner of the coal-mine and children were chained to coal carts or forced to crouch for hours deep underground, cramped, frozen and listless with boredom and hunger, opening and closing barriers to let the coal carts through.

Edinburgh life

In spite of the Union of the parliaments in 1707, when the centre of power shifted from Edinburgh to London, Scotland's capital city in the 18th century was full of life and vigour. The narrow streets were full of sedan chairs carried by Highland porters. The chairs were a necessity: the Old Town was awash with sewage. Gaelic greetings and curses mingled with the cries of street sellers, including fishwives from Newhaven and Musselburgh. Ladies in huge hoops influenced the design of the stairways —wrought-iron balustrades were curved out to accommodate them, one of which can be seen in Mylne's Court at the top of the Royal Mile. These ladies walked on red shoes with heels three inches high. They wore plaids about their shoulders and patches on their cheeks, while masks to conceal their identity were held close to their faces by string. Stately elderly women, faces well flushed from the 'ladies' refection' at 4 o'clock, tapped by on canes. They would rather pay a boy to light them home than be carried in a chair. Upright and strict, they were forthright and spoke in vigorous Scots.

Scottish painting flourished under the brush of Allan Ramsay (1718–84) and Henry Raeburn. There were women song-writers too: Lady Anne Lindsay, Jean Elliott (author of *The Flowers of the Forest*), Mrs Cockburn and Lady Nairne. And there were medical men like Dr Cullen, a physician whose large sand-glass for counting his patients' pulse beats bulged out under his coat flaps. There were judges in high wigs who carried their hats, and there was Lord Monbodo, author of a book called *The Origin of Language*, who, when it was wet, put his wig inside a sedan chair and himself walked home. (The first umbrella didn't appear until 1782 when it was carried by a surgeon, Alexander Wood.)

CHAPTER 7: THE HIGHLAND CLEARANCES

Martin Martin's observations show how people who lived by the sea also lived off the sea. Limpets, he noted, were used for bait and so was the 'short white down of goose'. It was fastened behind the hook, the boat was continually rowed, the fish chased after the down and were caught by spears which the fishermen held in his hand, bound firmly around with a rope. Limpets were parboiled using very little water and the broth was reported to be very beneficial for nursing mothers, while boiled whilks were 'a good remedy against stone'.

Lowland prejudice against the Gaelic-speaking people of Scotland is highlighted by the fact that a Gaelic-speaking minister was presumed to be able to speak Amerindian languages, as Professor Donald Meek explains:

American Indians represented the same sort of 'problem' as Highlanders and needed to be integrated into civilization as well as converted. In fact, the Indians and the Highlanders were so sharply focused together in the mind of the SSPCK that in 1735 the SSPCK despatched a Gaelic-speaking Highland minister called John MacLeod, a native of Skye, to Georgia where he was to serve Gaelic-speaking emigrants and preach to the Indians. Lurking behind this twin-track approach to ministry was (apparently) the view that Gaelic was related to the

Amerindian languages. We now know that this was not the case, but in the 18th century various misconceptions of this kind were entertained about the Celtic languages and those of other 'primitive' peoples. In the mind of the SSPCK, Gaelic and Amerindian languages were comparable in another way—they were equated with barbarism and incivility, and were to be 'worn out' and replaced with English as soon as possible.[116]

The full text of Dr Kennedy's attack on Episcopalian worship is as follows:

I entered a large building that seemed made for any purpose but that of hearing, with windows daubed over with paint, as if those who made them were afraid the light of heaven would come pure on the people who might meet within... in stalked a man who seemed to have come straight from his bed, for he had on his nightgown, which fortunately happened to be a long one. The poor man must have been crazy, for who in his senses would come in such a plight before a congregation. Turning towards the people he began to read some gibberish out of a book... All of a sudden he and they rose from their knees, and there came a sound like that of a pipe and fiddle together from behind me. I thought when I heard the music begin that the people had risen up to dance; but no, they stood quite still. On looking round I saw... a large box with long yellow whistles stuck in the front of it, from which came the noise. The deluded people, it seems, as they did not like to praise the Lord themselves, and were afraid not to get it done at all, set this box to make a noise through its whistles for them. But, by this time, I had more than enough of it; and, remembering it was the Lord's Day, I hurried out of the place, right glad to escape from the synagogue of Satan.

Another piece of anti-Highland prejudice is shown when the surveyor of James Riddell's property recommended importing contractors from Galloway and Ayrshire to see through the improvements 'as the people of Sunart and Ardnamurchan do not seem to be up to the business' (*The Riddell Papers*). *The Edinburgh Advertiser* reported the duel on 25 April 1783, in which Riddell's son died, as follows:

Yesterday morning a duel was fought in a field near Bayswater between Capt Riddell of the 2nd troop of Dragoon guards and Lieut Cunninghame of the Scots

Greys, when at first fire both gentlemen were unluckily shot through the body. We are sorry to acquaint our readers that Capt Riddell died of the wound he received in this most unfortunate affair at 7 o'clock this morning.

The paper explains:

Mr R and Mr C about three years ago had a difference. They met afterwards several times, but never in good humour: some offensive expressions had dropped from each party when they originally differed, and the recollections of them served to increase their mutual enmity. About five months ago, Mr R was induced to send Mr C a challenge and in consequence of some pointed observations that passed on the old subject… The meeting was fixed for Monday morning at 10 o'clock in a field on the right hand side of the Uxbridge Road, about a mile from Tyburn turnpike. They were both punctual; Mr R attended by Capt Topham of the Horse Guards… Eight paces were measured by the seconds and afterwards the contending parties took their ground… Mr R fired and shot Mr C under the right breast, the ball passing as it is supposed, through the ribs and lodging in the left side of the back. The moment Mr C received the shot he reeled but did not fall, opened his waistcoat and declared he was mortally wounded. Mr R still remained his ground and Mr C after a pause of 2 minutes declared he would not be taken off the field until he fired at his adversary. Mr C then presented his pistol, shot Mr R in the groin; he immediately fell and was carried in a hackney coach to Mr T's house, Portman Square. The unhappy gentleman lingered until 7 o'clock on Tues morning then expired… perhaps no young man was ever more regretted—many thousands shed tears for his loss and the conduct of Lt Cunningham was universally reprobated, from the King downwards, particularly for his taking a long aim and firing after he received a shot in consequence of a fair toss up for the first, and after acknowledging himself to be mortally wounded—only it was of a piece with his character.

Mr Riddell was interred on Friday 2nd May 1783 in a vault made on purpose in the south aisle of Westminster abbey nearby under Garrick's Monument, a little to the left. His uncle John Riddell was Chief Mourner and a number of friends followed in cloaks, and about 70 officers of different rank followed in their uniforms. The body was preceded by the clergy and choristers singing. The Cathedral was crowded with ladies of fashion and other people.[117]

The full text of Dr John MacLachlan's poem is as follows:

Dìreadh a-mach ri Beinn Shianta,
Gur cianail tha mo smuaintean,
A'faicinn na beinne 'na fàsach
'S i gun àiteach air a h-uachdar…
'S lìonmhor bothan bochd gun àird air
Air gach taobh 'nan làraich uaine,
Agus fàrdach tha gun mhullach
Is 'na thulaich aig an fhuaran.
Far an robh 'n teine 's na pàisdean,
'S ann as àirde dh'fhàs an luachair.
Far an cruinnicheadh na h-àrmainn,
Feuch a'chaora bhàn le h-uan ann.
Ach, fhir shanntaich rinn an droch-bheairt…
An dall, an seann duine, 's an òinid
Toirt am mallachd air do bhuaireas.
Smuaintich fhèin, nuair thèid thu null bhuainn,
Mar bheir Rìgh nan Dùl do dhuais dhut…
Bheil thu 'm dùil gum faigh thu saorsainn
Leis na caoraich 's do chuid bhuailtean?

'As I climb up towards Ben Shiant my thoughts are filled with sadness, seeing the mountain as a wilderness, with no cultivation on its surface. So many poor cottages in disarray, in green ruins on each side, and houses without a roof, in heaps by the water-spring.' Where the fire and children once were, that's where the rushes have grown tallest. Where the heroes used to gather, behold the white sheep and her lamb there! But, covetous perpetrator of the evil deed… the blind, the old, and the deranged heap their curses on your trouble-making. Just consider, when you pass from us, how the King of All will reward you… Do you think you will win deliverance because of your sheep and all your folds?'

The text and translation of John MacLean's poem is:

> Gur muladach mise 's mi an seo gun duin' idir
> A thogas, no thuigeas, no sheinneas leam dàn;
> Le dùrachd mo chridhe, soraidh slàn leis na gillean
> A sheòl thar na linne gu Manitobà...
> 'S nuair ràinig a' mhadainn gu dol air an aineol,
> 'S a thionail gach caraid a bh'aca san àit',
> Chan urra mi aithris am bròn a bh'air m'aire
> 'S an cùl ris a' bhaile sa mhadainn Di-màirt...
> 'S bidh innealan baoghalt' sa Ghàidhealtachd daonnan
> Gu fògradh nan daoine, 's cur chaorach 'nan àit'.

'How sad I am without a single companion who can raise, or understand, or sing a song with me; with all the goodwill of my heart, I bid a fond farewell to the lads who sailed over the ocean to Manitoba... When that morning came when they were to go to a strange land, and every friend in the place had gathered, I cannot express the sorrow that weighed me down as they turned their backs on the township on that Tuesday morning... The free-holders of land at this time are obsessed with dragging the world's riches away from the rest; and foolish devices will always be tried in the Highlands to disperse the people and put sheep in their place.'

Writing about 19th-century revivals and the eventual attempt by Highlanders to gain control of the land, Donald Meek writes:

It is fair to claim that the revivals helped to liberate the expression of the Gaelic people. Sermons, by ministers and laymen, became a major art form, as did prayers and hymns rooted in the Scriptures. Hymns, in particular, preserve a link with secular tradition by employing secular tunes and traditional genres of verse for spiritual ends. Like the Gaelic hymns, the revival movements themselves drew on traditional aspects of Gaelic life, most notably the corporate identity of the community, and helped to mould and reinforce that identity. It has been argued that one of the results of the 19th-century revivals was the growth of a strong, indigenous lay leadership which was able to direct the campaign for land reform in the 1870s and especially the 1880s. Local leaders… laced their speeches with allusions to the Bible which pointed to the liberation and vindication of God's people—a message which was bound to strike a chord in the minds of oppressed, but devout, Highlanders… Mary MacPherson of Skye, popularly known as 'Mairi Mhor nan Oran' ('Big Mary of the Songs')… made connections between the location of the 1841–42 revival meetings in Skye and the crofters' conventions, held forty years later, on the same spot, namely Fairy Bridge:

> Chunnaic sinn bristeadh na fàire
> Is neòil na tràillealachd air chall,
> And là a sheas MacCaluin làimh ruinn
> Aig Beul-àtha-nan-trì-allt.

'We saw the dawn breaking, and the clouds of thralldom put to flight, the day MacCallum stood beside us at Fairy Bridge.'[118]

CHAPTER 8: REVIVAL & MISSION IN THE 19TH CENTURY

Among the many stories of hardship endured by adherents to the breakaway Free Church is the following anecdote:

A laird from a nearby estate had been riding through Methven, in Perthshire, when a dog startled his horse. The laird shot the dog—but also blinded a little girl who was sitting on her doorstep close by. He gave the family a small piece of land in compensation. In her old age the woman offered this land to the Free Kirk. 'Others gae their siller,' she said, (others gave their silver, money) but she had offered her eye.[119]

The full text of Father Andrew Scott's tirade is:

If yer nae pleas't wi' the way I dae fer yer gude, what for dinna ye tak a sail to Rome, and see hoo ye come on at the Vatican, if ye ken whar that is; or, maybe, a lot of ye that's camstreery (unmanageable, obstinate) and bully-rag (wrangle) me here wad like to try the way that they dae in McLean's Kirk ower the water

there. The males and females, they tell me, a get in a word in eleckin' (electing)
their ministers and layin oot the siller; and that's what a pack o' ye wad want to
hae here—to meet, and spyke (speak), and jaw (yack), and instruc' me hoo to
dae we' this, and hoo to dae wi' that. But I'll tak care o' ye… This is a Catholic
Church, and I sall ever keep it sae, for nae ane o' ye I'll alloo to cheep. That's my
deceeshin (decision) for yer digestin' a' nicht.[120]

Chesterton's piece on George MacDonald is worth quoting in full:

The spiritual colour of Scotland, like the local colour of so many Scottish moors,
is a purple that in some lights can look grey. The national character is in reality
intensely romantic and passionate—indeed, excessively and dangerously
romantic and passionate. Its emotional torrent has only too often been turned
towards revenge, or lust, or cruelty, or witchcraft. There is no drunkenness like
Scotch drunkenness; it has in it the ancient shriek and the wild shrillness of the
Maenads in the mountains. And of course it is equally true on the good side, as
in the great literature of the nation… Nevertheless, by a queer historical accident
this vivid and colourful people have been forced to 'wear their blacks' in sort of
endless funeral on an eternal Sabbath…

Now, among the many men of genius Scotland produced in the 19th century,
there was only one so original as to go back to his origin. There was only one who
really represented what Scottish religion should have been, if it had continued the
colour of the Scottish medieval poetry. In his particular type of literary work he
did indeed realize the apparent paradox of a St Francis of Aberdeen, seeing the
same sort of halo around every flower or bird. It is not the same thing as any
poet's appreciation of the beauty of the flower or bird. A heathen can feel them
and remain heathen, or, in other words remain sad. It is a certain special sense
of significance, which the tradition that most values it calls sacramental. To have
got back to it, or forward to it, at one bound of boyhood, out of the black Sabbath
of a Calvinist town, was a miracle of imagination.

James Young Simpson invited two colleagues to help him experiment with
chloroform. James kept his drugs tucked away in a small cupboard in the
dining room within the wooden window casings. It can still be seen today.
At the end of the meal, tumblers of chloroform were brought in. The three

doctors inhaled deeply, passed out and, to the alarm of the servants, toppled under the dining-room table—characteristically, James recovered first.

CHAPTER 9: MISSION & CARE IN THE 20TH CENTURY

The trip in memory of Jane Haining is organized by Queen's Park Church. Miss Jean Bain sent details of the programme and a report written by a group from the church, adults and young people, who visited Budapest in 1996:

At 6.30pm we left Queen's Park church in Glasgow by coach for Heathrow Airport where we were to catch a plane bound for Budapest. We were all very excited as many of us had never flown before and had not been out of the UK before.

Our flight to Budapest arrived in at 9.30 am and the Revd Susan Cowell from the Scottish Mission was there to meet us. We were transported to our hotel by coach where we were allowed an hour to unpack. Then followed our week of non-stop action… We were amazed at the warmth of the welcome we received from everyone and at the fact that even some of the youngest children could speak some English… Everyone was very aware of the differences between their own school experiences and the morning spent in school in Hungary… As this was the school where our Church missionary, Jane Haining, worked and looked after Jewish girls during the war, we were able to see for ourselves the room where she would have lived and the dungeon where she hid the Jewish girls from the Gestapo. This was opened up specially for our visit and the present school staff had never been in it. The dark, dismal, cramped conditions that these children lived in shocked us.

Here are some facts on the Church of Scotland's care programmes.

The Church of Scotland's Board of Social Responsibility cares for people in need every day of the year, irrespective of religious affiliation. The 1600 staff, from gardeners to directors, must be Christians—though not necessarily members of the Church of Scotland. A housing association in Glasgow recently challenged the Kirk's stance, asking if it were realistic in a mainly Muslim area. But it is seen as vitally important for the Church to maintain its Christian basis. 'The foundation stone for all our work continues to be to offer a service in Christ's name,' writes Mrs Ann Allen, the Convener of the Board of Social Responsibility.

The Church's drugs counselling service includes a family support group for people who are affected by past or present drug use of another member of the family. Talk, art and role-play all contribute to the support. Listening and sharing are equally important. 'It provided me with a safe environment for the release of my own emotions,' one person said. Staff also provide a counselling and groupwork service to Scottish prisons. Services are free and confidential and personally tailored to meet the unique needs of each individual. The aim is holistic, helping people to look at deep-rooted issues which may be the underlying cause of their actions, helping people to develop self-awareness, self-worth and confidence.

CHAPTER 10: LOST FOR WORDS

Because language has been a theme throughout this book and is one which is not generally discussed by theologians or preachers (although they use words), I feel it is vital to pay attention to ideas raised by Fearghus MacFhionnlaigh, and I want to conclude this Appendix by giving a fuller extract from his thought-provoking essay:

It seems to me that Christians make a fundamental mistake when they understand the confusion of language at Babel as a curse... My burden is that God has delivered humanity from the thraldom of Babel by giving us many languages. The single language was the curse—the multiplicity of languages was the blessing.

God's commission to mankind through Adam was of course 'Be fruitful and multiply. Fill the earth and subdue it' (Genesis 1:28). The impulse of Babel was directly counter to that. It was a centripetal rather than a centrifugal force. It promised unity, but it was an impacted absolute unity. Freedom is only possible where there is choice...

The light of God floods the black skyscraper of Babel. It becomes a crystal— a prism of colours exploding in all directions. (Remember the transparent be- jewelled New Jerusalem). Each refracted colour (each language!) is a search- light. Not like the search-lights of a prison-camp spotlighting escapees in order that they may be shot down, but tunnels of coloured light acting as corridors of escape. And the fugitives are not escaping from God—they are escaping into God. For Christ is the True Ziggurat, the True Staircase, the True Door, the True Route of Escape, the True Light, the True Word. Only in him do our words have meaning. To him who overcomes Christ will give a 'white stone with a new name written on it, known only to him who receives it' (Revelation 2:17). To each a personal name (word? language? identity?) of God-given, God-filled meaning, rock-solid meaning. The Second Adam is the true name-giver…

God leads the jailbreak. For freedom Christ has set us free, free to seek God while he may be found and where he may be found (though he is not far from any of us). And each language is a search-light with which to seek him. A fissure, a hole punched in the wall of silence.

The essay ends with a plea for action 'before the silence steps closer':

Cursed is the ground because of our disobedience. Did not God make Adam steward of the earth? Are we not stewards still? Are we not stewards also of the languages we speak? … are we not stewards in particular of the languages unique to our own nations? And if the saying 'It is not the healthy but the sick who need the doctor' holds good culturally also, then where should the attentions of the linguistically-called Scot be? … One of those beams of light from Babel is called Scottish Gaelic. It is flickering and fading. It was in our stewardship but we have neglected it. If it goes out there will be one less route of escape for mankind. One less window through which to look for and find God. Let us act. Before the light fails. Before the wisdom dies. Before the silence steps closer.

Christ is Lord of all. And should we the messengers fall mute, the very stones will cry out! As to what language they will speak, well…!

NOTES

1   Quoted in *The Triumph Tree: Scotland's Earliest Poetry AD550–1350*, edited Thomas Owen Clancy, Canongate Classics, 1998.

2   Quoted in Michael Lynch, *Scotland, A New History*, Pimlico, 1992.

3   John and Winifred MacQueen, *The Miracles of Bishop Nynia*, PolygonCosmos, 1990.

4   Ruth and Frank Morris, *Scottish Healing Wells*, The Althea Press, 1982.

5   Andrew Patterson, *A Way to Whithorn*, Saint Andrew Press, 1993.

6   MacQueen, *The Miracles of Bishop Nynia*.

7   *The Triumph Tree*.

8   *The Triumph Tree*.

9   Adamnan, *Life of St Columba*, Llanerch Enterprises, 1988.

10 Pinkerton, *Enquiry*, quoted by William Reeves, Preface to Adamnan's *Life of St Columba*, Llanerch, 1988.

11 Adamnan, *Life of St Columba*.

12 Gaelic MS, displayed in Edinburgh at an exhibition by St Mark's Coptic Church, September 2000.

13 Quoted in *The Days of the Fathers in Ross-shire, 1861*, John Kennedy, Christian Focus Publications, 1979.

14 Dallan Forgaill, 'Elegy for Colum-Cille', in *The Triumph Tree*.

15 Forgaill, 'Elegy for Colum-Cille', in *The Triumph Tree*.

16 These facts come from William Dalrymple, *From the Holy Mountain*, Flamingo, 1989; also from Maire Herbert, 'The Bible in Early Times' in David F. Wright (ed), *The Bible in Scottish Life*, St Andrew Press, Edinburgh 1988.

17 *The Triumph Tree*.

18 *The Triumph Tree*.

19 Martin MacGregor, 'Church and Culture in the Late Medieval Highlands', in James Kirk, ed., *The Church in the Highlands*, The Scottish Church History Society, 1998.

20 Ian Finlay, *Columba*, Gollancz, 1979.

21 Facts and quotes from Ron Ferguson, *Chasing the Wild Goose*, Fount, 1988.

22 Facts from the *Church Times* 15 and 22 October 1999.

23 Facts from Andrew Patterson, *A Way to Whithorn*.

24 Sally M. Foster, *Picts, Gaels and Scots*, Batsford, 1996.

25 Sir David Lyndsay, quoted in *Restalrig Parish Church*, Revd Robert Black Notman BD, Society of Friends of Restalrig Church, 1976.

26 Alan Wilson, *St Margaret, Queen of Scotland*, John Donald Publishers Ltd, 1993.

27 John Knox, *History of the Reformation in Scotland* (spelling modernized), quoted in *Mary Queen of Scots: The Scottish Setting*, The Education Department, National Galleries of Scotland.

28 Wilson, *St Margaret, Queen of Scotland*.

29 Quoted by Robert Wright, 'Viewpoint', *The Financial Times*, 10 November 1999.

30 'St Stephen's Admonitions to his Son', quoted Wilson, *St Margaret, Queen of Scotland*.

31 Quoted Wilson, *St Margaret, Queen of Scotland*.

32 Quoted Wilson, *St Margaret, Queen of Scotland*.

33 *Life of St Margaret, Queen of Scotland*, Bishop Turgot, from *Ancient Lives of Scottish Saints*, Alexander Gardner, Floris Books, 1993.

34 Quoted Kay Jamieson, *An Unquiet Mind*, Picador, 1997.

35 *The Triumph Tree*.

36 A.P. Forbes, *Kalendars of Scottish Saints*, Edinburgh, 1872.

37 Quoted Andrew Monaghan, *God's People?* Saint Andrew Press, 1991.

38 Facts from Andrew Monaghan, *God's People?*.

39 Ian B. Cowan, *The Medieval Church in Scotland*, Scottish Academic Press, 1995.

40 Composed by Aithbhreac inghean Coirceadail for Niall MacNeill of Gigha, quoted Martin MacGregor in 'Church and Culture in the Late Medieval Highlands'.

41 Wedderburn Brothers, *Gude and Godlie Ballatis*, quoted David F. Wright, 'The Bible in the Scottish Reformation' in *The Bible in Scottish Life and Literature*, St Andrew Press, 1988.

42 Quoted Sarah Carpenter, 'The Bible in Medieval Verse and Drama' in *The Bible in Scottish Life and Literature*.

43 J.A.W. Bennett, *Devotional Pieces in Verse and Prose* from MS Arundel 285 and MS Harleian 6919, Blackwood, 1955 (author's translation).

44 *The Triumph Tree*.

45 Quoted Stewart Lamont, *The Life of Saint Andrew*, Hodder and Stoughton, 1997.

46 David Wright, ed., *The Bible in Scottish Life and Literature* (spelling modernized and anglicized).

47 Breadalbane papers, quoted Cowan, *The Medieval Church in Scotland*.

48 D.P. Thompson, *Women of the Scottish Church*, St Andrews Press, 1975.

49 Quoted Thomas Torrance, *Scottish Theology*, T&T Clark, 1996 (spelling modernized).

50 Quoted Wright, *The Bible in Scottish Life and Literature*.

51 Robin Bell, *Bittersweet Within My Heart*, Pavilion, 1992, quoted Sarah M. Dunnigan, 'Scottish Women Writers c. 1560–1650' in Gifford and McMillan, eds., *A History of Scottish Women's Writing*, Edinburgh University Press, 1997.

52 'History of the Roman Catholic Church from the Reformation in 1560 to the Present Day', course paper.

53 Quoted Torrance, *Scottish Theology* (spelling modernized).

54 John Buchan, *Montrose*, Thomas Nelson & Sons, 1931.

55 Cameron, Wright, Lachman, Meek (eds.), *Dictionary of Scottish Church History and Theology*, T&T Clark, 1993.

56 Quoted Cameron et al., *Dictionary of Scottish Church History and Theology*.

57 Quoted in many accounts, including D.P. Thomson, *Women of the Scottish Church*.

58 Quoted in many accounts, including D.P. Thomson, *Women of the Scottish Church*.

59 Biggar Museums Trust.

60 Quoted Donald Meek, 'The Reformation and Gaelic Culture' in James Kirk, ed., *The Church in the Highlands*.

61 Donald Meek, *The Scottish Highlands, the Churches and Gaelic Culture*, WCC Publications, 1996.

62 Henry Grey Graham, *The Social Life of Scotland in the Eighteenth Century*, Black, 1901.

63 Quoted in *Source Book of Scottish History*, Volume 3, Nelson.

64 Graham, *The Social Life of Scotland in the Eighteenth Century*.

65 Alec Forbes, *George MacDonald*, quoted Michael R. Phillips, *George MacDonald*, Bethany House Publishers, 1987.

66 John Kennedy, *The Days of the Fathers in Ross-shire*.

67 Agnes Keith, *The Parish of Drainie and Lossiemouth*, publisher, 1975.

68 Cameron et al., *Dictionary of Scottish Church History and Theology*.

69 Quoted Arthur Fawcett in *The Cambuslang Revival*, Banner of Truth Trust, 1971. All subsequent references to Cambuslang come from this source, spelling modernized.

70 Quoted Ross Roy in 'The Bible in Burns and Scott', in Wright, ed., *The Bible in Scottish Literature*.

71 Fawcett, *The Cambusland Revival*.

72 Lynch, *Scotland, a New History*.

73 Quoted Fawcett, *The Cambuslang Revival*.

74 Quoted Grey Graham, *The Social Life of Scotland in the Eighteenth Century*.

75 Grey Graham, *The Social Life of Scotland in the Eighteenth Century*.

76 Cameron et al., *Dictionary of Scottish Church History and Theology*.

77 John Carsewell, *The Epistle to the Reader, 1567*, quoted Donald Meek, 'The Gaelic Bible', in Wright ed., *The Bible in Scottish Life and Literature*.

78 Alasdair Roberts, 'Roman Catholicism in the Highlands', in Kirk ed., *The Church in the Highlands*.

79 Lynch, *Scotland, A New History*.

80 Kennedy, *The Days of the Fathers in Ross-shire*.

81 Hunter, *Making of the Crofting Community*, John Donald, 2000.

82 Hunter, *Making of the Crofting Community*.

83 Hunter, *Making of the Crofting Community*.

84 Riddell Papers, Register House, Edinburgh.

85 Riddell Papers.

86 Donald Meek ed., trs., *Tuath is Tighearna (Tenants and Landlords)*, Scottish Academic Press, for the Scottish Gaelic Texts Society, 1995.

87 *Twelve Days in Skye*, London 1852. All quotations from Hunter, *Making of the Crofting Community*.

88 Lynch, *Scotland, a New History*.

89 Kennedy, *The Days of the Fathers in Ross-shire*.

90 Meek trs., *Tenants and Landlords*.

91 *The Days of the Fathers*.

92 Donald Macleod, *The Gospel in the Highlands*, Lewis Recordings, March 1995.

93 Annual Reports of the Highland Missionary Society, 1824.

94 Quoted Douglas Ansdell, *The People of the Great Faith*, Acair, 1998.

95 Quoted Donald Meek, 'The Gaelic Bible, Revival and Mission' in Kirk ed., *The Church in the Highlands*.

96 Quoted Meek, in Kirk ed., *The Church in the Highlands*.

97 Facts from Professor Alec McCheyne, *Dictionary* and Lynch, *Scotland, a New History*.

98 All quotations Andrew Bonar, *Robert Murray McCheyne*, Banner of Truth, reprinted 1997.

99 Quoted John MacLeod, *Bypaths of Highland Church History*, Knox Press, 1966.

100 Facts and quotes from Anthony Ross, OP, *The Development of the Scottish Catholic Community 1878–1978*, unpublished paper.

101 C.S. Lewis, *George MacDonald: An Anthology*, quoted Michael Phillips, *George MacDonald*, Bethany House Publishers, 1987.

102 Phillips, *George MacDonald*, p. 345.

103 Phillips, *George MacDonald*, p. 165.

104 Quotes from Thomson, *Women of the Scottish Church*.

105 Cameron, Wright, Lachman, Meek eds., *Women of the Scottish Church and Dictionary of the Scottish Church History*, T & T Clark, 1993.

106 Dictionary.

107 Quotes and information from Derick Forrest, *Sir James Young Simpson*, Simpson House, October 1997.

108 Monaghan, *God's People*.

109 Monaghan, *God's People*, and Felicity O'Brien, *The Cheerful Giver*, St Paul Publications, 1989.

110 Ian Alexander, *Church of Scotland World Mission*, CSWM, 1998.

111 These figures come from Mark Dilworth OSB.

112 Stewart Lamont, *The Life of Saint Andrew, Apostle, Saint and Enigma*, Hodder and Stoughton, 1997, quoted by Ruth Gledhill *The Times*, 30 November 2000.

113 *The Scotsman*, 7 December 2000.

114 *Scottish Bulletin of Evangelical Theology*, Volume 14 Number 1, Spring 1996.

115 Attributed to Revd Dr Stuart Wauchope, 1930.

116 Donald Meek, *The Scottish Highlands*, WCC Publications, 1996.

117 *Edinburgh Advertiser* and *Edinburgh Courant*, National Library of Scotland.

118 Meek, 'The Gaelic Bible, Revival and Mission', in Kirk ed., *The Church in the Highlands*.

119 Thompson, *Women of the Scottish Church*.

120 Ross, *The Development of the Scottish Catholic Community 1878–1978*.

ACKNOWLEDGMENTS

We would like to thank all those who have given us permission to include quotations in this book, as indicated in the list below. Every effort has been made to trace and acknowledge copyright holders of all the quotations included. We apologize for any errors or omissions that may remain, and would ask those concerned to contact the publishers, who will ensure that full acknowledgment is made in the future.

Text and translation of 'Dìreadh a-mach ri Beinn Shinta' by Dr John MacLachlan, and of 'Manitoba' by John MacLean, from *Tuath is Tighearna*, ed. Professor Donald Meek ed., Scottish Academic Press, used by permission of The Scottish Gaelic Texts Society. Extracts from Adamnan's *Life of Saint Columba* used by permission of Llanerch Enterprises. Extracts from *The Triumph Tree: Scotland's Earliest Poetry AD550–1350*, ed. Thomas Owen Clancy, used by permission of Canongate. Extracts from *The Cambuslang Revival* by Arthur Fawcett, and *Robert Murray McCheyne* by Andrew Bonar, used by permission of The Banner of Truth Trust. Extracts from *Dictionary of Scottish Church History and Theology*, eds. Cameron, Wright, Lachman and Meek, used by permission of T&T Clark Ltd.

You may be interested to know that Jenny Robertson is a regular contributor to *New Daylight*, BRF's popular series of Bible reading notes. *New Daylight* is ideal for those looking for a fresh, devotional approach to reading and understanding the Bible. Each issue covers four months of daily Bible reading and reflection with each day offering a Bible passage (text included), helpful comment and a prayer or thought for the day ahead.

New Daylight is written by a gifted team of contributors including Adrian Plass, Margaret Cundiff, David Winter, Rob Gillion, Graham Dodds, Peter Graves, Helen Julian CSF, David Spriggs, Jenny Robertson and Veronica Zundel.

New Daylight is also available in large print and on cassette for the visually impaired.

NEW DAYLIGHT SUBSCRIPTIONS

❑ I would like to give a gift subscription
(please complete both name and address sections below)
❑ I would like to take out a subscription myself
(complete name and address details only once)

This completed coupon should be sent with appropriate payment to BRF. Alternatively, please write to us quoting your name, address, the subscription you would like for either yourself or a friend (with their name and address), the start date and credit card number, expiry date and signature if paying by credit card.

Gift subscription name _____

Gift subscription address _____

_____ Postcode _____

Please send to the above, beginning with the September 2001/January 2002 issue:

(please tick box)	UK	SURFACE	AIR MAIL
NEW DAYLIGHT	❑ £10.50	❑ £11.85	❑ £14.10
NEW DAYLIGHT 3-year sub	❑ £26.50		

Please complete the payment details below and send your coupon, with appropriate payment to: **BRF, First Floor, Elsfield Hall, 15–17 Elsfield Way, Oxford OX2 8FG**

Your name _____

Your address _____

_____ Postcode _____

Total enclosed £ _____ (cheques should be made payable to 'BRF')

Payment by cheque ❑ postal order ❑ Visa ❑ Mastercard ❑ Switch ❑

Card number: ⬚⬚⬚⬚⬚⬚⬚⬚⬚⬚⬚⬚⬚⬚⬚⬚⬚⬚⬚⬚

Expiry date of card: ⬚⬚⬚⬚   Issue number (Switch): ⬚⬚⬚⬚

Signature (essential if paying by credit/Switch card)_____

NB: BRF notes are also available from your local Christian bookshop.   **BRF is a Registered Charity**

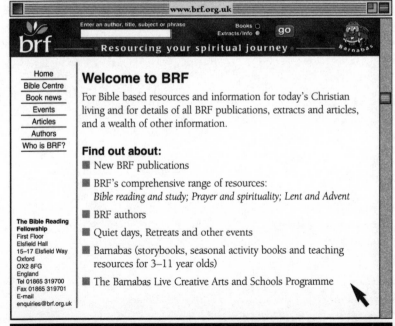

www.brf.org.uk

Enter an author, title, subject or phrase

Books ○
Extracts/Info ●

go

brf

Resourcing your spiritual journey

Barnabas

- Home
- Bible Centre
- Book news
- Events
- Articles
- Authors
- Who is BRF?

The Bible Reading Fellowship
First Floor
Elsfield Hall
15–17 Elsfield Way
Oxford
OX2 8FG
England
Tel 01865 319700
Fax 01865 319701
E-mail
enquiries@brf.org.uk

Welcome to BRF

For Bible based resources and information for today's Christian living and for details of all BRF publications, extracts and articles, and a wealth of other information.

Find out about:

■ New BRF publications

■ BRF's comprehensive range of resources:
 Bible reading and study; Prayer and spirituality; Lent and Advent

■ BRF authors

■ Quiet days, Retreats and other events

■ Barnabas (storybooks, seasonal activity books and teaching resources for 3–11 year olds)

■ The Barnabas Live Creative Arts and Schools Programme

Visit the BRF website at www.brf.org.uk

BRF is a Registered Charity